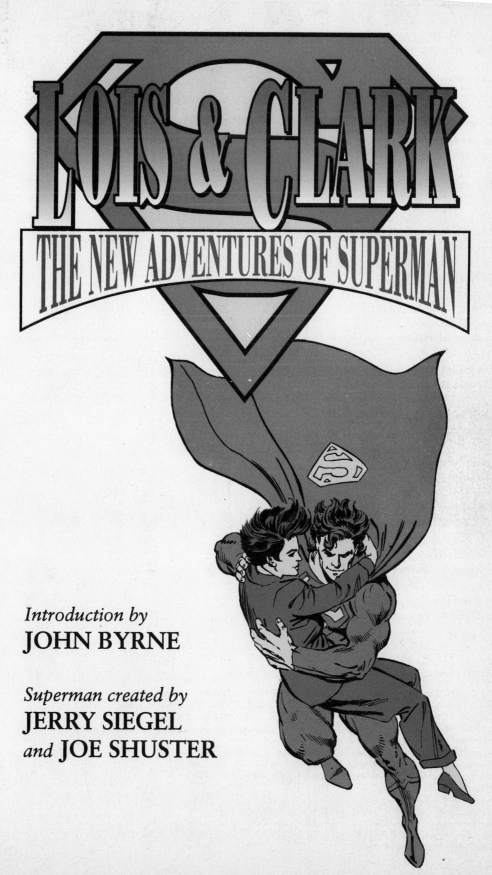

LOIS & CLARK

THE NEW ADVENTURES OF SUPERMAN

Introduction by
JOHN BYRNE

Superman created by
JERRY SIEGEL
and **JOE SHUSTER**

LOIS AND CLARK, THE NEW ADVENTURES OF SUPERMAN

Published by DC Comics. Cover and compilation copyright © 1994 DC Comics. All Rights Reserved.
Originally published in single magazine form in MAN OF STEEL 2, SUPERMAN ANNUAL 1, SUPERMAN
9,11, ACTION COMICS 600,655 and ADVENTURES OF SUPERMAN 445, 462 AND 466. Copyright ©
1986, 1987, 1988 and 1990 DC Comics. All Rights Reserved. All characters, their distinctive likenesses and related
indicia featured in this publication are trademarks of DC Comics.
The stories, characters, and incidents featured in this publication are entirely fictional.
DC Comics, 1325 Avenue of the Americas, New York, NY 10019
A division of Warner Bros. - A Time Warner Entertainment Company
Printed in Canada. First Printing.
ISBN: 1-56389-128-X
Front cover photograph courtesy Jerry Fitzgerald, Warner Bros. Television.
Back cover photograph courtesy Bob D'Amico, ABC.
Logo courtesy Warner Bros. Television.
Publication design by Veronica Carlin

CONTENTS

LOIS & CLARK

AN INTRODUCTION

by John Byrne

I used to wonder when he'd done it; when Superman had been so foolish as to announce to the world that he had a secret identity, a place to which he retired when he wasn't out there fighting for truth, justice and the American way.

It must have been fairly early on, I decided, since Lana Lang, Superboy's red-headed girlfriend back in Smallville, seemed to devote her every waking hour to some scheme directed toward tricking Clark Kent into revealing he was Superboy, or vice versa. (Seen in this light, Lois Lane did no more than inherit Lana's mantle.) Still, it made for a curious bump in the otherwise smooth carpet of the legend, at least as I saw it when I was ten years old.

So, when did Superman reveal he had a secret identity?

Of course, he never did. Rather, this is one of the more obvious examples of Superman being endangered by the only people on earth who truly had the power to destroy him: his editors and writers. They knew his dual identity and so, almost without conscious thought, somewhere along the way the existence of that closely guarded secret, if not the secret itself, became public coin.

It's difficult to trace the exact moment at which the first domino toppled — a story was done in the early sixties (if memory serves) titled "When Lois First Suspected Clark Was Superman," but this was written to play off the existing motif — but it had become so ingrained that when I was invited, in 1985, to submit a proposal for a "revamp" of Superman, the idea of completely abolishing this notion seemed almost sacrilegious. Not, perhaps, the most controversial thing I did in the two years I piloted Superman's ship of state – leaving Ma and Pa Kent alive in Superman's adulthood seemed to be that — but one that stretched across the whole fabric of his creation.

It seemed a very simple thing, really. Since I was instructed to start the whole Superman Mythos over again, from day one, it was easy enough to omit this timeworn tradition. The fact that "my" version of Superman would never have donned the familiar costume until he came to Metropolis as an adult (as it had been in the original version, created by Jerry Siegel and Joe Shuster), there would be no preestablished framework of suspicion. When Superman debuted in Metropolis, the world simply assumed it was his first appearance anywhere and — more important – that he was Superman all the time.

(For those not intimately conversant with the Superman Mythos, a bit of history might come in handy right about now. Above I make references to Lana Lang, Smallville and Superboy, all elements quite familiar to many who read these words. Yet, only a few lines later, I state that the creators of Superman introduced him as an adult, in Metropolis. The apparent contradiction here is part of the nature — the strangely elastic nature — of comics. When Siegel and Shuster created their Man of Tomorrow he did, indeed, begin his career full grown, as Superman. It was not until several years later that Superboy was retrofitted to the growing Legend, in his own title, with Superman proudly introducing his youthful adventures on the cover. Nowadays, a change of this nature would send continuity-conscious fans into fits of apoplexy, but the world was a simpler place in those days, and the addition of Superboy simply meant more Super-material every month. No one complained.)

It was only logical, when any kind of thought was given to the matter, that Superman would have the easiest time of any super-hero convincing the world, almost subliminally, that there was no need to search for his Alter Ego. Batman, Green Lantern, the Flash — in fact, virtually all the other heroes of the "DC Universe" wore masks, and made it obvious thereby that they were concealing something. Superman wore no mask, and it was not logical to assume he donned one in his civilian guise. Therefore, no civilian guise; when Superman was not patrolling the skies over Metropolis, he was probably off in Botswana or Outer Mongolia or somewhere. (Much is made of Clark's ability to completely disguise himself by the simple exercise of putting on a pair of glasses. When I got glasses for the first time, when I was 12, I did not expect my friends to fail to recognize me, and, indeed, most of the actors who have portrayed the characters have done little to dispel the apparent absurdity of the cliché. For me, though, it was Christopher Reeve who convinced me there was more than a comic-book contrivance at work in Clark's disguise. By altering his hair and posture — which Superman also did in the comics — and adopting a pair of glasses that, by their size and configuration, subtly altered the shape of his face, Chris made me *believe* Superman's disguise could work.)

Making the decision to eliminate worldwide awareness that Superman had a secret identity, as I've noted, had a far-reaching effect on the shape of the Myth. Mostly, it altered the characters and relationship of Lois and Clark.

Poor Lois. When she'd been introduced back in 1938 she'd been glamorous, tough, resourceful, fully in charge of her own life and career. (I've often wondered if some part of her did not come from *His Girl Friday*, from Rosalind Russell's portrayal of Hildy Johnson, a perfect template for Lois.) She was a little reckless, sometimes, but she'd survived before Superman arrived on the scene, and it would be reasonably safe to assume she would have continued to survive without him.

Unfortunately, she would not stay that way. By the fifties, when I first "met" Lois, she had changed considerably. The role of women in society had changed, and

Lois mirrored this. When the Boys came marching home from the war they expected the Girls to march back into the kitchen, and with very few exceptions they did. Those exceptions, "Career Women" as they came to be called, were seen as aberrations, and when they found their way into fiction they usually fitted a single mold: bitter, frustrated, left eternally empty and unsatisfied by their decision to abandon the "correct" role of wife and mother. Lois became a prime example of this: no matter that she was the best reporter — or "girl reporter," since one had to qualify these things — on the *Daily Planet*, she would never be satisfied, never be whole until she had (a) tricked Clark into revealing he was Superman and (b) won from this marriage to the Man of Steel.

I cannot say what readers thought of Lois when she was introduced in the first issue of *Action Comics*, but I know how we felt about the woman she'd become by the fifties — we hated her. The extraordinary misogynist picture painted of her (and to a slightly lesser extent, the young Lana) embodied everything boys hated about girls. (Remember when boys hated girls? When they didn't figure out that the relationship was supposed to be something else until they hit puberty? Simpler times, simpler times.) Lois was nosy, clinging, inefficient — a royal pain in the butt. And a long fall from 1938.

But the simple exercise of eliminating global knowledge that Superman had a dual identity changed all that. In one fell swoop Lois was restored to something like her former glory. No more prying. No more scheming. She looked at Clark Kent and saw — Clark Kent. Only Clark Kent. And, in the version I assembled, Clark was someone Lois started out resenting. He beat her to the exclusive on Superman. That was how he got his job at the *Planet*. And that was something for which Lois would never forgive him.

Well — maybe never.

Clark was totally smitten with Lois from the moment he first met her. As a small-town boy — albeit, by then, a well-traveled small-town boy — he still nurtured certain ideas of what a woman should be, and Lois was so much more. Glamorous, yes, but more than that. She demanded — and got — equal footing in what was traditionally a men's club, the newsroom of a major newspaper. She asked no special treatment because she was "only a girl," and none was forthcoming. She had won her position by proving she was as good as the best. How could Clark not fall for her?

It was the counterpoint to Lois's reaction to Superman. I began with the assumption that "my" Lois had a perfectly normal, perfectly healthy love life before Superman showed up. She'd just never found quite what she was looking for. Until Superman. In him she saw the prize she'd sought: as she had striven for no less than the best in every other aspect of her life, so too she wanted no less in love. But there was more than a cold, calculated "He's-Number-One-So-I-Must-Have-Him" attitude. After all, in the revised version Lex Luthor was the richest, most powerful man on earth before Superman arrived (his criminal nature was now more subtle, not a surface attribute — and, following a brain transplant [this *is* comics] he is a younger, sexier Lex)) and Lois had managed to resist his charms, as other women had not. But as Clark was genuinely smitten with Lois, so Lois fell utterly and unapologetically in love with Superman.

Thus was created what has been so aptly dubbed "A Triangle Built for Two." In the past, Clark never had a chance with Lois. She had eyes only for Superman and, in those rare moments when she was not devoting her energies to revealing Clark to be Superman, she felt nothing but pity for her newsroom coworker — how could he be the best in the business and still be such a wimp? (It was in those occasional stories that Lois showed her softer side — when she hatched schemes not designed to strip Superman of his secret, but to boost Clark's minuscule self-esteem.) In the new, improved (really the original) form, Clark was free to pursue Lois on his own terms. It was important to him that he win her as Clark, as a human being, not as an icon.

In this fashion another of the cornerstones of the former relationship was turned inside out. The main dynamic of the triangle had been a kind of sneering, adolescent revenge fantasy: Lois might scoff at Clark, but that was her loss, since by doing so she robbed herself of the inside track to Superman. There wasn't a preteen boy on earth who could not plug into that – "You think I'm just a pimply-faced loser, but if you knew my *secret*...."

Now, though, it was *important* to Clark that he convince Lois of his real worth, his human worth. After all, Clark Kent was who he really was, who he'd been most of his life. Superman was just a red and blue suit he wore. He wasn't a real person. That was Clark, the boy raised in Smallville, the man trying to carve a life for himself in Metropolis. A life in which the most important element was a vivacious young woman named Lois Lane.

A life most ably represented in Superman's latest foray into another medium, this time TV again with *Lois and Clark: The New Adventures of Superman*. Even the title tells us something more than the old Lois-as-pain-in-the-butt/Superman-as-square-jawed-hero routine. It's about two people finding each other, discovering the dynamics of their relationship.

In other words, it's about everything I've come to think of as making these characters *matter*.

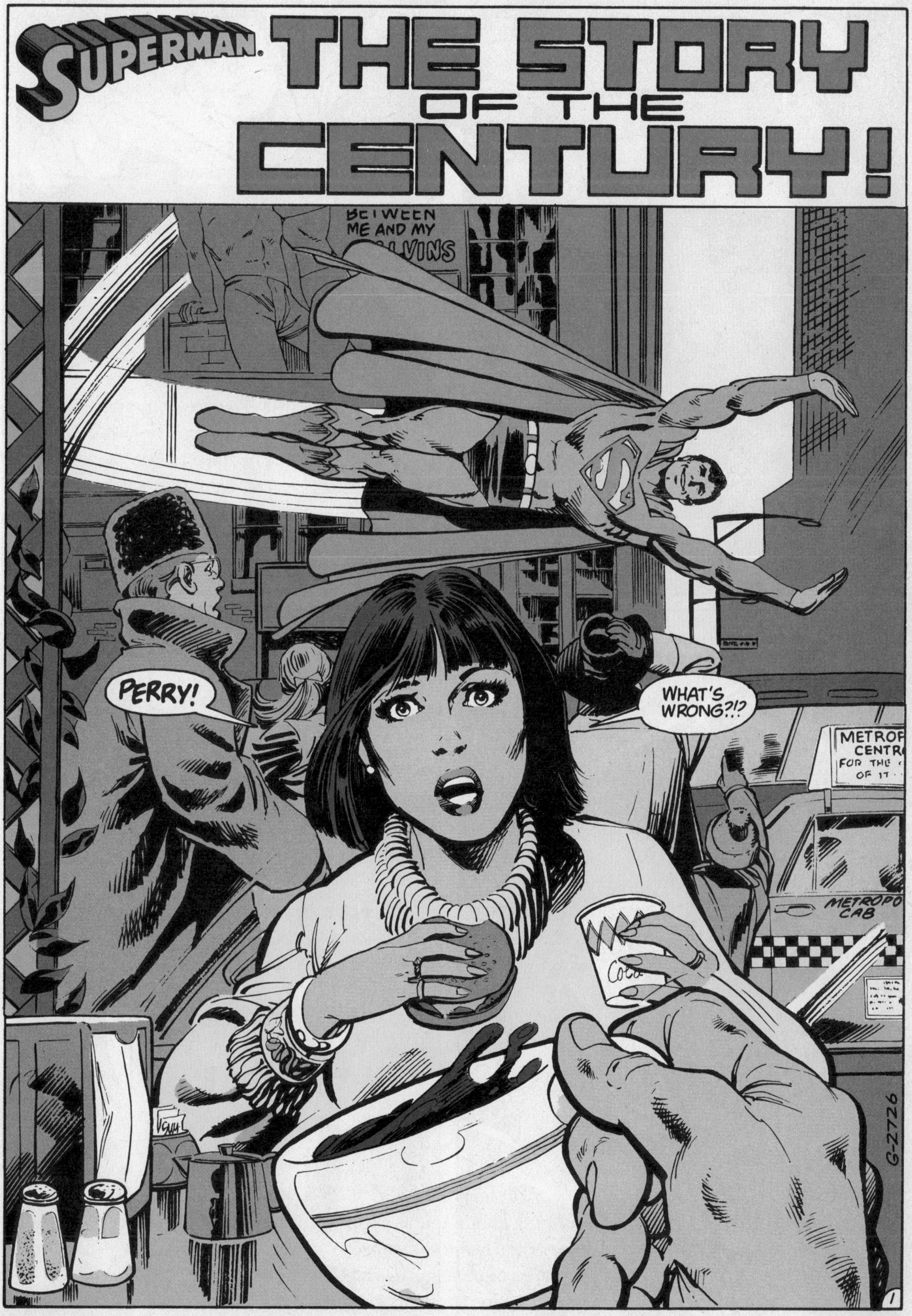
SUPERMAN
THE STORY OF THE CENTURY!
BETWEEN ME AND MY CALVINS
PERRY!
WHAT'S WRONG?!?
METROPO CENTR FOR THE OF IT
METROPO CAB
G-2726
1

OMIGOSH!! IT'S *HIM*!!

IT'S *HIM*!!!

YOU'RE SURE? THAT'S THE *"SUPERMAN"* WHO SAVED THAT CRASHING SPACE PLANE?

IT MUST BE!

HE'S CHANGED HIS *OUTFIT*, BUT WHEN WAS THE LAST TIME YOU SAW A FLYING MAN IN *METROPOLIS*?

THEN GET AFTER HIM, LOIS! STAY WITH HIM NO MATTER WHAT HAPPENS!

GET ME THAT *STORY!!*

AS GOOD AS GOT, CHIEF! TELL THE RE-WRITE BOYS TO STAY CLOSE TO THEIR PHONES--

--*LOIS LANE* IS ON THE JOB!!

THERE SHE IS, BOSS.

JUST LIKE YOU *PREDICTED*.

OF COURSE. STOP THE CAR AND CALL HER OVER, *GUTHRIE*.

MISS LANE! YO, MISS LANE!

MISTER L WANTS TO SEE YOU.

GUTHRIE! TELL YOUR BOSS I'M BUSY!

YOU CAN TELL 'IM YOURSELF, MISS LANE. HE'S RIGHT *HERE*.

LOOK, SPARE ME THE CONFRONTATION, WOULD YOU? I'M IN A MAJOR HURRY, AND *LEX* CAN ALWAYS CATCH UP TO ME *LATER*.

BUT--BUT MISS LANE, HE'S LEAVIN' FOR *SOUTH AMERICA* THIS EVENIN'. HE WON'T BE 'BACK FOR AT LEAST A *YEAR!*

THEN HE'LL HAVE TO CATCH ME *MUCH* LATER. SEE YOU!

BLAST! BLAST! BLAST! BLAST! *BLAST!*

THERE'S NO *SIGN* OF HIM. JUST THAT HALF-SECOND DELAY, AND HE'S *DISAPPEARED!*

WELL, *SAM LANE'S* OLDEST DAUGHTER ISN'T BEATEN *THAT* EASILY.

HI, *SID?* HI, IT'S LOIS.. IS *CHUCK* AROUND? I HAVE A SLIGHTLY *HUGE* FAVOR TO ASK...

TEN MINUTES LATER...

NUTS! I STILL DON'T *SEE* HIM!

NO SURPRISIN', LOIS. THIS FLYIN' MAN OF YOURS AIN'T LIKE A *PLANE.*

HE COULD BE DOWN IN THEM CANYONS 'TWEEN THE BUILDINGS, AN' YOU'D *NEVER* SPOT 'IM FROM UP HERE.

MAYBE. MAYBE. HIT THE *POLICE BAND.* THERE MIGHT BE SOMETHING COOKING THAT'LL LURE MY FRIEND OUT OF HIDING.

4

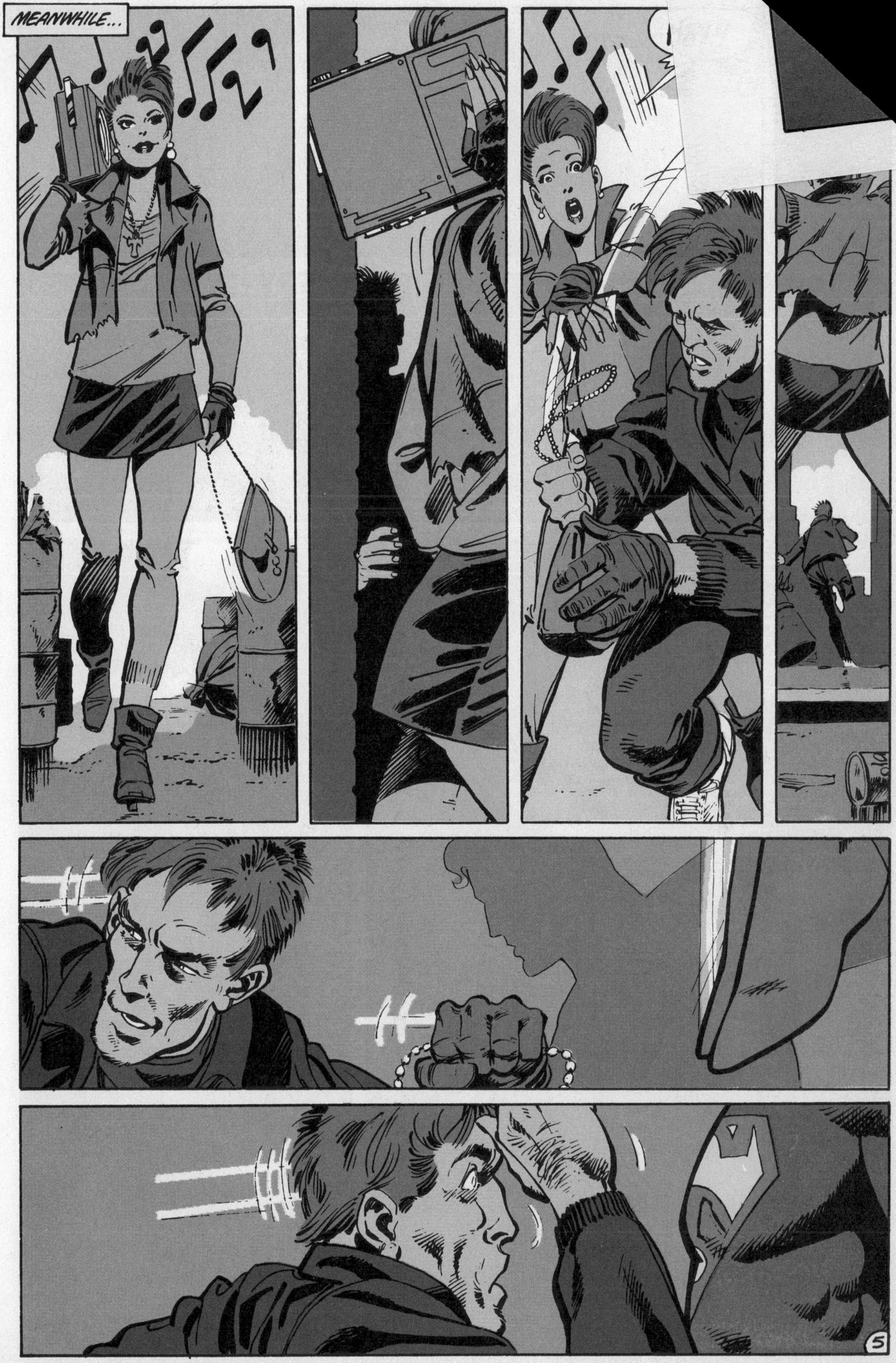
MEANWHILE...
5

YOU DON'T *REALLY* WANT TO STEAL THAT YOUNG WOMAN'S PURSE, DO YOU?

SHE DOESN'T LOOK AS IF SHE HAS MUCH MORE MONEY TO SPARE THAN YOU.

HA-MANNA HA-MANNA HA-MANNA

AND SO...

OH, MISS...?

OGOD OGODOGOD OGODOGOD OGODOGOD!

6

I BELIEVE *THIS* BELONGS TO YOU...?

...INTERRUPT THIS PROGRAM FOR AN IMPORTANT *NEWS BULLETIN.*

POLICE HAVE SURROUNDED *CLANCY'S LIQUOR STORE* ON EAST FIFTIETH STREET, WHERE FOUR ARMED GUNMEN ARE KNOWN TO BE HOLDING AT LEAST THREE PERSONS HOSTAGE...

YOU'LL BOTH HAVE TO EXCUSE ME, NOW. THAT SOUNDS LIKE SOMETHING A LITTLE MORE UP MY ALLEY.

LET ME JUST MAKE CERTAIN OUR FRIEND HERE DOESN'T *STRAY* TOO FAR...

HELP KEE METROPO CLEA DON'T LIT

YEOWP!

...BY HANGING HIM FROM THIS LAMP POST.

HEY! PUMME *DOWN!*

THAT SHOULD HOLD HIM UNTIL YOU CAN CALL THE POLICE AND PRESS CHARGES.

OH... AND I THINK THAT RADIO IS A *TRIFLE LOUD,* DON'T YOU?

AFTER ALL, IN A CITY THIS *SIZE,* CONSIDERATION FOR OTHERS IS THE ONLY THING THAT KEEPS LIFE *BEARABLE.*

'BYE, NOW!

MEANWHILE... NOW HEAR THIS! YOU IN THE STORE! THIS IS CAPTAIN REAGAN, OF THE SPECIAL WEAPONS AND TACTICS SQUAD!

I'M GIVING YOU JUST ONE MINUTE TO COME OUT.

AND YOU CAN START RELEASING THE HOSTAGES NOW.

WINES AND BEERS

LIQUOR

WINES AND BEERS

IN YOUR EAR, PIG! YOU COME ONE STEP CLOSER...

...AND WE'LL START DECORATING THIS STORE WITH THESE PEOPLE'S BRAINS!

DAMN!

I WAS KINDA HOPING MY REPUTATION WOULD BE ENOUGH TO SCARE THEM OUTTA THERE.

GUESS NOT, SKIPPER. LOOKS LIKE WE'LL REALLY HAVE TO GO IN AFTER 'EM.

BUT THERE ARE BOUND TO BE CIVILIAN CASUALTIES...

MAYBE NOT. LET ME HELP.

HUH? WHAT IN THE NAME OF...?

WHAT CIRCUS DID YOU ESCAPE FROM??

NO CIRCUS, CAPTAIN. WILL YOU ASK YOUR MEN TO PULL BACK, PLEASE?

I DON'T WANT TO RISK THEM GETTING HIT BY STRAY BULLETS.

8

"STRAY...?"

WHO DO YOU THINK...

HEY! COME *BACK* HERE!

JUST DO AS I *ASK*, PLEASE, CAPTAIN. BELIEVE ME, IT WILL MAKE YOUR LIFE MUCH *EASIER*.

JUST HOLD IT RIGHT THERE, PRETTY BOY.

ONE MORE STEP AND YOU'RE *DOG-FOOD!*

OH, COME *ON* NOW.

WHAT ARE YOU *AFRAID* OF? YOU DON'T THINK I'M HIDING ANY WEAPONS IN *THIS* OUTFIT, DO YOU?

NO... I...

HEY! I SAID HOLD IT!

I SAID HOLD IT!

HOLD IT!

HEY!

KRIMP!

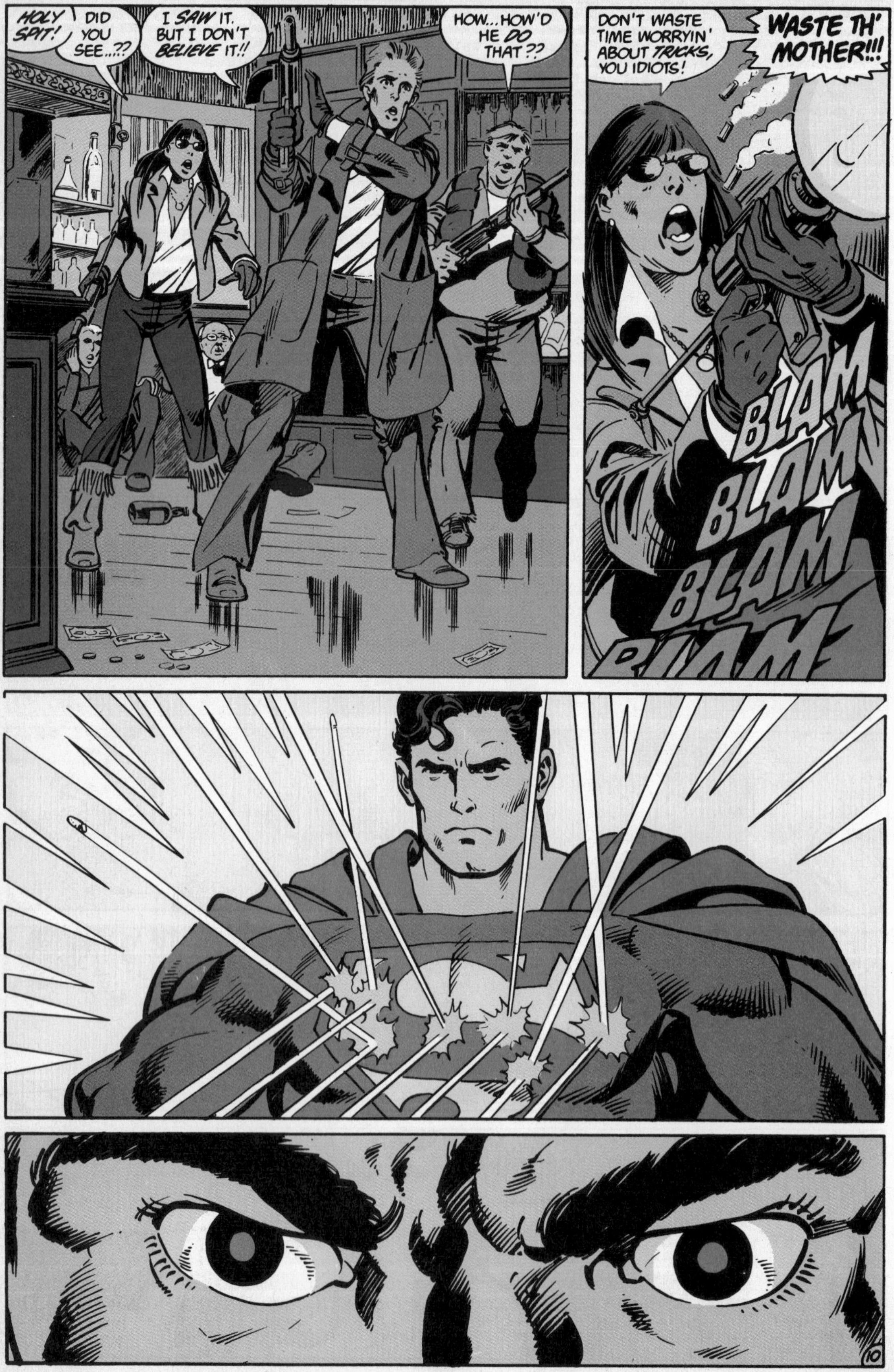

HOLY SPIT!
DID YOU SEE...??
I SAW IT. BUT I DON'T BELIEVE IT!!
HOW...HOW'D HE DO THAT??
DON'T WASTE TIME WORRYIN' ABOUT TRICKS, YOU IDIOTS!
WASTE TH' MOTHER!!!
BLAM BLAM BLAM BLAM
10

HE--HE AIN'T *HUMAN!!*

HIS *EYES!* WHAT'S HAPPENIN' TO HIS *EYES?!?*

HEY! MY GUN! IT'S GETTIN'...

HOT!!

AND NOW...

A COUPLE OF MY *SOFTEST* TAPS...

...AND YOU CREEPS SHOULD BE IN *DREAMLAND* FOR ABOUT AN HOUR.

NOW, THEN...

Y-Y-YOU WOULDN'T HIT A *LADY*..

...WOULD YOU...?

11

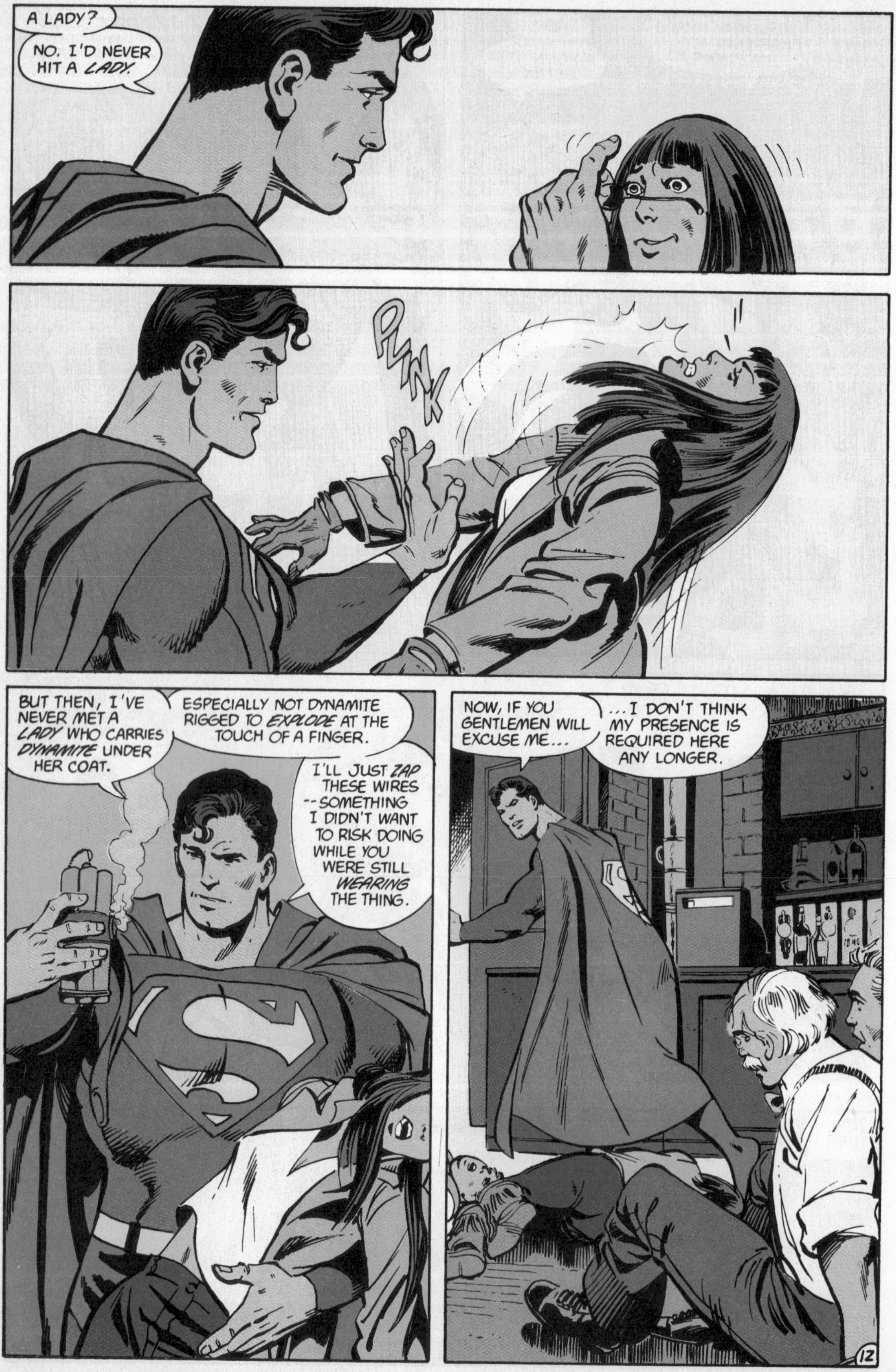
A LADY?
NO. I'D NEVER HIT A LADY.
PLINK
BUT THEN, I'VE NEVER MET A LADY WHO CARRIES DYNAMITE UNDER HER COAT.
ESPECIALLY NOT DYNAMITE RIGGED TO EXPLODE AT THE TOUCH OF A FINGER.
I'LL JUST ZAP THESE WIRES --SOMETHING I DIDN'T WANT TO RISK DOING WHILE YOU WERE STILL WEARING THE THING.
NOW, IF YOU GENTLEMEN WILL EXCUSE ME...
...I DON'T THINK MY PRESENCE IS REQUIRED HERE ANY LONGER.
12

MEANWHILE... THERE'S THE PLACE, LOIS. JUST LIKE THEY SAID ON THE RADIO.

GREAT! GET DOWN CLOSE TO ONE OF THOSE ROOFTOPS SO I CAN JUMP OUTTA THIS BEAST.

"JUMP...?" ARE YOU NUTS, WOMAN??

JUST DO IT, CHUCK. I DIDN'T WIN MY PULITZER PRIZE BY SITTING IN FRONT OF A WORD PROCESSOR ALL DAY.

AND SO... CATCH YOU LATER, PAL.

AND THANKS!

JUST DON'T GET KILLED, LOIS. MISTER L WOULD HAVE MY HIDE IF HE THOUGHT I'D HELPED YOU DO THAT!

I'M SURE HE WOULD, TOO.

I GUESS LEX LUTHOR IS A SITUATION I REALLY MUST ADDRESS, ONE OF THESE DAYS.

AFTER ALL, HE IS THE MOST POWERFUL MAN IN METROPOLIS.

OR IS THAT "USED TO BE"?

AND, HIS ATTENTIONS ARE VERY FLATTERING.

BUT I'M JUST NOT IN THE MARKET FOR WHAT HE'S SELLING.

CAPTAIN REAGAN! AM I IN TIME?

LOIS LANE! THEN MY GUESS WAS RIGHT! THAT WAS THE MYSTERY "SUPERMAN" YOU DID THAT PIECE ON LAST WEEK.

THEN, HE'S HERE?

HE WAS. TOOK OFF JUST A FEW SECONDS AGO.

AND IN THE DAYS THAT FOLLOW...

SORRY, MISS LANE...

...HE *WAS* HERE...

...BUT YOU JUST...

...MISSED HIM.

HI, MISS LANE! I...

G-GOLLY! WHAT'S WRONG? YOU LOOK MISERABLE!

AND WHY SHOULDN'T I, JIMMY?

I'VE SPENT THE BETTER PART OF A WEEK CHASING OUR MYSTERY MAN ALL OVER METROPOLIS...

...AND ALL I'VE GOT TO SHOW FOR MY TROUBLE IS SORE FEET.

AND JUST TO ADD INSULT TO INJURY-- LOOK AT THIS! THE OTHER PAPERS HAVE PICKED UP ON MY "SUPERMAN" REFERENCE.

I'VE MANAGED TO NAME THE GUY, WITHOUT EVEN KNOWING WHO HE IS!!

EAGLE

UPERMAN OPS SUBWAY

SAVES WOMAN FALLEN ON TRACKS

WHO IS THE SUPERMAN?

METROPOLI

SUPERM FOILS ARMOR CAR HEIST!

ARTIST'S RENDERING

MYSTERY SUPER-HERO VANISHES AGAIN

JEEPERS, THAT'S ROUGH, MISS LANE.

TOO BAD YOU CAN'T FIND A WAY TO BE ON THE SPOT BEFORE HE GETS THERE.

YEAH. WELL, UNTIL I BECOME CLAIRVOYANT, THE ONLY WAY I CAN DO THAT IS TO...

TO...

HMMMMMMM...

15

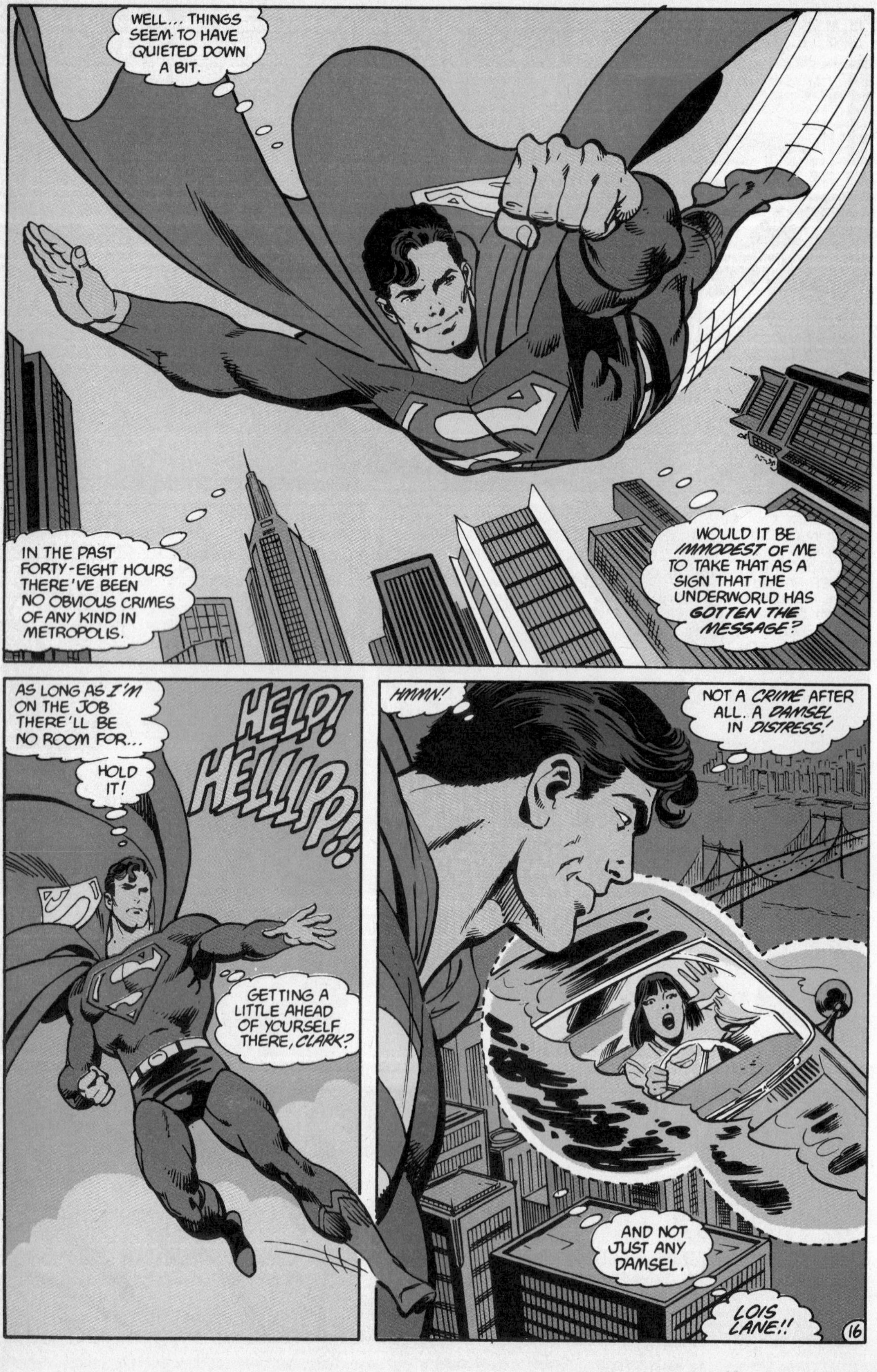
WELL... THINGS SEEM TO HAVE QUIETED DOWN A BIT.
IN THE PAST FORTY-EIGHT HOURS THERE'VE BEEN NO OBVIOUS CRIMES OF ANY KIND IN METROPOLIS.
WOULD IT BE IMMODEST OF ME TO TAKE THAT AS A SIGN THAT THE UNDERWORLD HAS GOTTEN THE MESSAGE?
AS LONG AS I'M ON THE JOB THERE'LL BE NO ROOM FOR...
HELP! HELLLP!!
HOLD IT!
GETTING A LITTLE AHEAD OF YOURSELF THERE, CLARK?
HMMN!
NOT A CRIME AFTER ALL. A DAMSEL IN DISTRESS!
AND NOT JUST ANY DAMSEL.
LOIS LANE!!
16

THAT LOOKS LIKE IT MUST BE THE SPOT WHERE HER CAR WENT OFF THE END OF THE PIER.

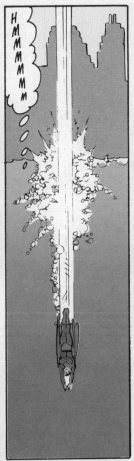

HMMMMM

17

23

THERE YOU GO. ARE YOU ALL RIGHT, MISS LANE?

A BIT WATER-LOGGED...

...BUT OTHERWISE, FINE. THANKS TO *YOU!*

DON'T MENTION IT. BUT IT'D PROBABLY BE WISE IF YOU GOT INTO SOME *DRY* CLOTHES AS SOON AS YOU CAN.

HERE, LET ME *FLY* YOU HOME.

OH-HHH!

YOU... KNOW WHERE I *LIVE*...?

OF COURSE, MISS LANE. I KNOW WHERE *EVERYONE* LIVES.

THERE. NOW, IF YOU'LL FORGIVE MY DASHING OFF, THERE ARE OTHER MATTERS I NEED TO ATTEND TO.

TAKE CARE NOW.

YEAH...

...ER...'BYE...ER...

HEY!

NO! WAIT!

COME BACK HERE!!!

YES...?

LATER...

18

24

THANKS AGAIN FOR WAITING WHILE I CLEANED MYSELF UP A BIT.

...ER, I THOUGHT WE MIGHT HAVE A LITTLE *SNACK*. SOME WHITE WINE AND BRIE...?

WELL, I HOPE YOU WON'T THINK ME TOO UNGRATEFUL, MISS LANE...

...BUT I DON'T *DRINK*, GENERALLY SPEAKING.

AND I NEVER REALLY ACQUIRED A *TASTE* FOR BRIE.

YOUR LOSS. IT'S ONE OF LIFE'S GREAT *PLEASURES*.

NOW, WHERE WERE WE?

FROM WHAT I'VE PICKED UP, YOU CAN *FLY*--YOU'RE VERY, VERY *FAST*--YOU CAN *SEE THROUGH ANYTHING*--AND YOU HAVE SOME KIND OF HEAT-RAY *ZAP* IN YOUR EYES...

... WHICH ARE *BLUE*.

YES... BUT AS I'VE ALREADY SAID, MISS LANE, I DON'T THINK KNOWING ALL THIS WILL BE OF MUCH USE TO YOU.

YOU'RE TOO *MODEST*. YOU HAPPEN TO BE THE STORY OF THE CENTURY, MISTER...

MISTER... ER... JUST *WHAT DO* WE CALL YOU, BY THE WAY?

I THINK THE NAME *YOU* GAVE ME IS QUITE *APPROPRIATE*, MISS LANE.

"SUPERMAN"?

ALL RIGHT, SUPERMAN IT IS! NOW, IS THERE ANY WAY I CAN GET YOU TO CALL ME *"LOIS"*?

OF COURSE. I'D BE DELIGHTED, LOIS.

(19)

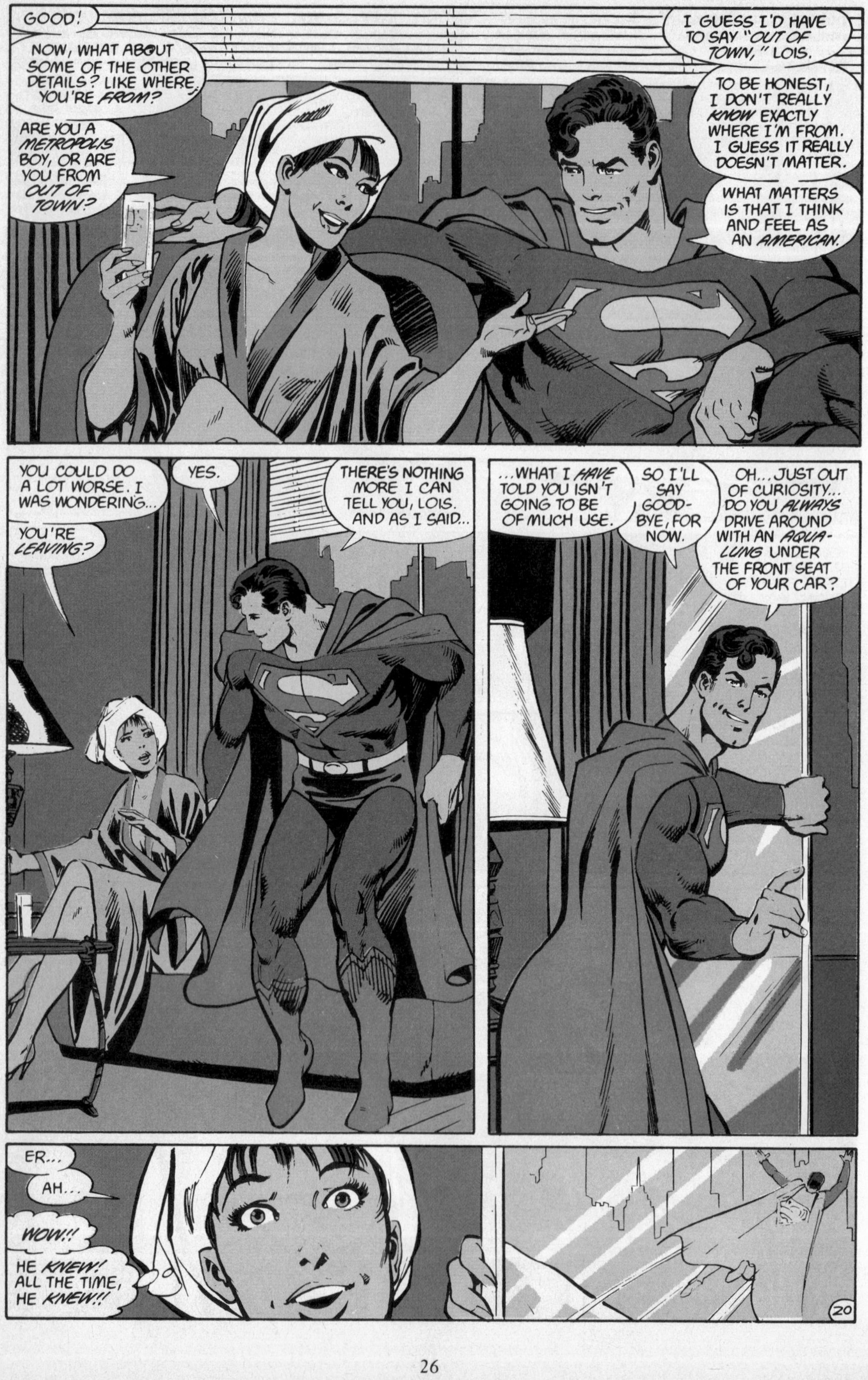
GOOD!
NOW, WHAT ABOUT SOME OF THE OTHER DETAILS? LIKE WHERE YOU'RE FROM?
ARE YOU A METROPOLIS BOY, OR ARE YOU FROM OUT OF TOWN?
I GUESS I'D HAVE TO SAY "OUT OF TOWN," LOIS.
TO BE HONEST, I DON'T REALLY KNOW EXACTLY WHERE I'M FROM. I GUESS IT REALLY DOESN'T MATTER.
WHAT MATTERS IS THAT I THINK AND FEEL AS AN AMERICAN.
YOU COULD DO A LOT WORSE. I WAS WONDERING...
YES.
YOU'RE LEAVING?
THERE'S NOTHING MORE I CAN TELL YOU, LOIS. AND AS I SAID...
...WHAT I HAVE TOLD YOU ISN'T GOING TO BE OF MUCH USE.
SO I'LL SAY GOOD-BYE, FOR NOW.
OH... JUST OUT OF CURIOSITY... DO YOU ALWAYS DRIVE AROUND WITH AN AQUA-LUNG UNDER THE FRONT SEAT OF YOUR CAR?
ER...
AH...
WOW!!
HE KNEW! ALL THE TIME, HE KNEW!!
20

SHE'S QUITE A WOMAN, LOIS LANE. *QUITE* A WOMAN! AND QUITE A *REPORTER*, TOO!

IMAGINE, *DELIBERATELY* DRIVING HER CAR OFF A PIER, JUST TO LURE ME IN FOR AN INTERVIEW.

GOOD THING I WASN'T ON THE OTHER SIDE OF THE *WORLD* AT THE TIME.

I DIDN'T NOTICE A *RESCUE CREW* STANDING BY, AND AN AQUA-LUNG AS SMALL AS THE ONE SHE HAD IN THE CAR WOULD HAVE RUN OUT BY THE TIME I HEARD HER CALLS FOR HELP...

...IF I EVER *DID*, AT SUCH RANGE.

I SUPPOSE I SHOULD GET AROUND TO TESTING THE *LIMITS* OF MY *SUPER-SENSES* ONE OF THESE DAYS.

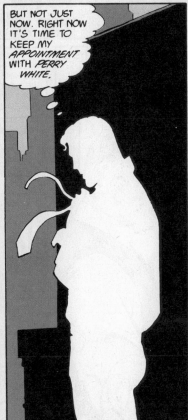

BUT NOT JUST NOW. RIGHT NOW IT'S TIME TO KEEP MY *APPOINTMENT* WITH *PERRY WHITE.*

THE APPOINTMENT I MADE *TWO DAYS AGO* AS *CLARK KENT!*

21

TWO HOURS LATER...

MISS LANE! DIDJA *HEAR?* THE CHIEF JUST HIRED...

LATER, JIM. I'VE GOT BIG FISH TO FRY!

STOP THE PRESSES, PERRY!! I'VE GOT THE STORY ON *SUPERMAN!*

WHAT?? LOIS, DIDN'T YOU PICK UP THE MESSAGE I LEFT ON YOUR ANSWERING MACHINE?

MESSAGE...?

NO. I DIDN'T CHECK MY MESSAGES. I WAS TOO BUSY WRITING THIS STORY...?

HEY, IS IT *ME,* OR DO I DETECT A LACK OF *EXCITEMENT* OVER THIS *SUPER-SCOOP?*

SORRY, LOIS. I KNOW HOW HARD YOU'VE WORKED FOR THIS, BUT I CAN'T GET ALL WOUND UP...

THE EXCLUSIVE STORY ON SUPERMAN

...OVER A STORY WE *ALREADY HAVE!!*

"ALREADY HAVE...?"

ALREADY HAVE??!?

RELAX, LOIS. RELAX. YOU WERE *BEATEN TO IT,* THAT'S ALL. HAPPENS TO THE *BEST* REPORTERS. USED TO HAPPEN TO ME ALL THE TIME.

PERRY WHITE MANAGING EDITOR

AND YOU MIGHT AS WELL TAKE A GOOD LOOK AT THE FELLA WHO GOT THE SUPERMAN STORY AHEAD OF YOU.

HE'S JOINED THE PLANET STAFF, AS OF TODAY.

LOIS LANE, MEET CLARK KENT!

Is there a fear greater than the fear born in ignorance? The fear that does not compre-hend itself? The <u>pain</u> that lies forever beyond the reach of understanding?

I have looked into eyes filled with such fear, <u>mindless</u> fear, <u>consuming</u> fear. And for the first time I <u>truly</u> understand what it is to be the helpless victim of a world gone <u>mad</u>.

They called him "<u>Titano</u>" -- something of a joke, I suppose, to his captors, his <u>tormentors</u>.

This is his story.

REALLY, *MISS LANE!* YOUR *PROTESTS* ARE QUITE WITHOUT FOUNDATION.

OUR WORK HERE IS *NECESSARY* AND *IMPORTANT.*

IMPORTANT?

IMPORTANT ENOUGH TO PUT SOME POOR *BEAST* THROUGH SIXTEEN DIFFERENT KINDS OF *HELL?*

The man in charge was <u>Thomas Moyers</u>. An eminent scientist. A man I'd met <u>before</u>...

...and learned to <u>hate</u>.

DON'T PLAY *INNOCENT* WITH ME, DOCTOR.

I KNOW WHERE THE *BODIES* ARE BURIED.

YOU'RE ONLY A *FREE MAN* TODAY BECAUSE YOU OFFERED *KITTY FAULKNER'S* DISCOVERIES TO THE *PENTAGON.*

MISS LANE...

LOOK AROUND YOU.

LOOK AT THE *OPENNESS* WITH WHICH WE CONDUCT OUR EXPERIMENTS.

THE *MINIMUM SECURITY* SURROUNDING THIS ESTABLISHMENT. DOES IT LOOK LIKE A *MILITARY* OPERATION TO YOU?

I tried to listen. All I could hear was Titano screaming...

THAT SOUNDS LIKE *DOUBLE-BLIND* TALK TO ME, DOCTOR.

I'M SUPPOSED TO THINK YOU'RE ON THE *UP-AND-UP* JUST BECAUSE YOU'RE NOT TRYING TO *HIDE* WHAT YOU'RE DOING?

I WONDER WHAT THE PEOPLE OF *METROPOLIS* WOULD HAVE TO SAY ABOUT IT, IF THEY KNEW YOU WERE MESSING WITH THESE KINDS OF *POWER LEVELS...*

...RIGHT IN THE *MIDDLE* OF OUR FAIR CITY!

TUT, TUT, MISS LANE!

YOU'RE TOO *INTELLIGENT* A WOMAN TO THREATEN ME WITH SUCH GROUNDLESS FEAR-MONGERING.

YOU KNOW PERFECTLY WELL THE *BLAST SHIELDS* WE'VE INSTALLED IN THIS FACILITY WOULD CONTAIN ANY UNEXPECTED RELEASE OF ENERGY.

AND, AS YOU CAN PLAINLY SEE, YOUR ALTRUISM IS QUITE MISPLACED.

TITANO IS PERFECTLY ALL RIGHT.

IS HE?

I'VE SEE PRIZE-FIGHTERS THAT LOOKED BETTER AFTER LOSING TWELVE ROUNDS.

EASY, MONKEY, EASY, BOY.

HE'S GROGGY, TO BE SURE. BUT YOU CAN TAKE MY WORD FOR IT, MISS LANE...

IF ANYTHING, TITANO IS NOW BETTER THAN HE WAS BEFORE WE BEGAN.

REALLY?

A PITY WE CAN'T GET HIS ASSURANCE OF...

HEY!!

LOOK OUT!!

SKREEK!! SKREEEK!!

BLAST IT!

I THOUGHT YOU HAD HIM!

OH, OF ALL THE...

RESTRAIN HIM! MILLER! DOBBS! DON'T JUST STAND THERE!

STOP HIM!!

HEY!!

THAT'S EASIER SAID THAN DONE, DOC!

HE SHOULD BE TOTALLY ZONKED OUT...

BUT HE'S FASTER THAN EVER!

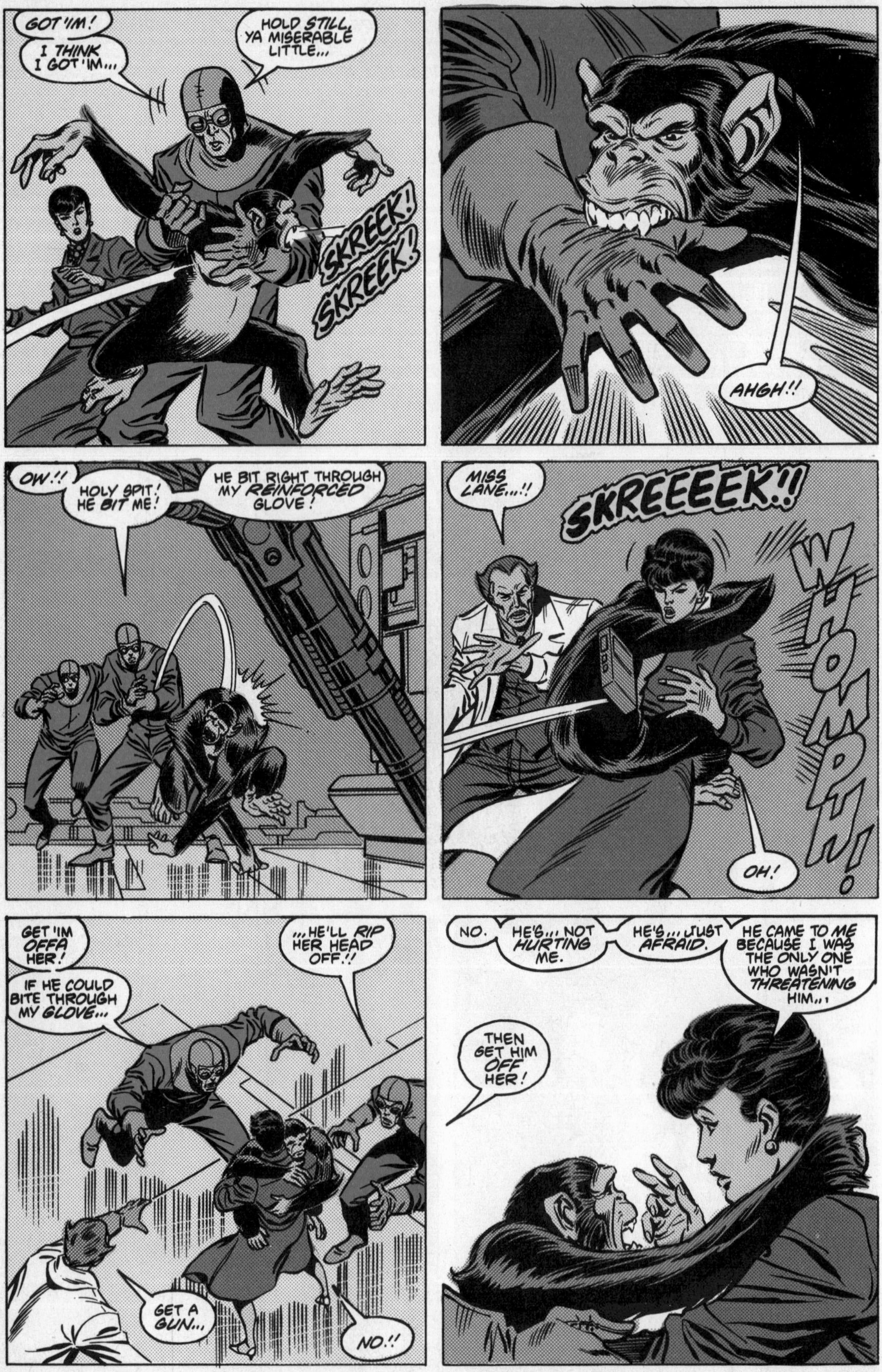
GOT 'IM!
I THINK I GOT 'IM...
HOLD STILL, YA MISERABLE LITTLE...
SKREEK! SKREEK!
AHGH!!
OW!!
HOLY SPIT! HE BIT ME!
HE BIT RIGHT THROUGH MY REINFORCED GLOVE!
MISS LANE...!!
SKREEEEK!!
WHOMPH!
OH!
GET 'IM OFFA HER!
IF HE COULD BITE THROUGH MY GLOVE...
...HE'LL RIP HER HEAD OFF!!
GET A GUN...
NO!!
NO.
HE'S... NOT HURTING ME.
HE'S... JUST AFRAID.
HE CAME TO ME BECAUSE I WAS THE ONLY ONE WHO WASN'T THREATENING HIM...
THEN GET HIM OFF HER!

WAIT! WHAT ARE YOU GOING TO DO!?!

GET HIM TO A HOLDING CHAMBER.

WE'LL CONTINUE THE EXPERIMENT!

Y-YESSIR!

HOLD 'IM!

HOLD 'IM!

SHREEEKK

AND AS FOR YOU, MISS LANE...

I THINK THIS INTERVIEW IS CONCLUDED!

MRS. WALLER, WOULD YOU ESCORT MISS LANE OUT OF HERE...?

YES, DOCTOR.

NOW JUST A DARNED MIN--

YOU HEARD THE DOCTOR.

TIME FOR YOU TO LEAVE.

DON'T GET PUSHY, CHUBS. THIS ISN'T JUST ONE REPORTER YOU'RE MESSING WITH...

THIS IS...

THE DAILY PLANET!!

SLAM!

I walked away. Angry. Frustrated.

And swearing that whatever else happened, this was not over yet!

I had no idea how right I was.

33

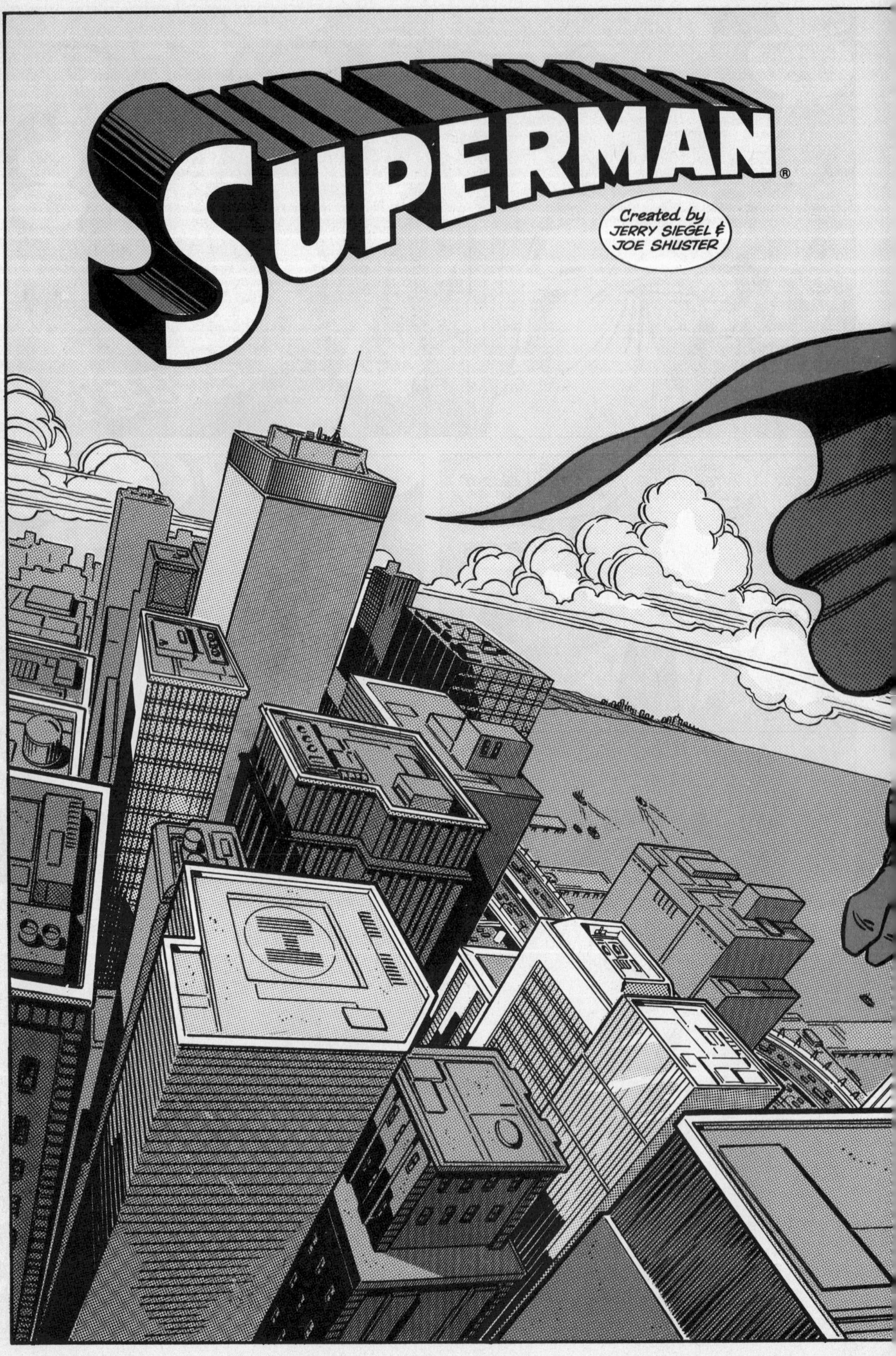
SUPERMAN®
Created by
JERRY SIEGEL &
JOE SHUSTER

TEARS FOR TITANO!

THIS IS THE *LIFE!*

CLEAN SKIES. SUMMER WEATHER.

AND THE WORST *CRIME* WITHIN RANGE OF MY *TELESCOPIC VISION* IS A LITTLE OLD LADY *JAYWALKING* OVER ON BLEEKER.

JOHN BYRNE- SCRIPTER / CO-PLOTTER
RON FRENZ- PENCILLER / CO-PLOTTER
BRETT BREEDING -- EMBELLISHER
ALBERT T. DE GUZMAN- LETTERER
TOM ZIUKO- COLORIST
MIKE CARLIN- EDITOR

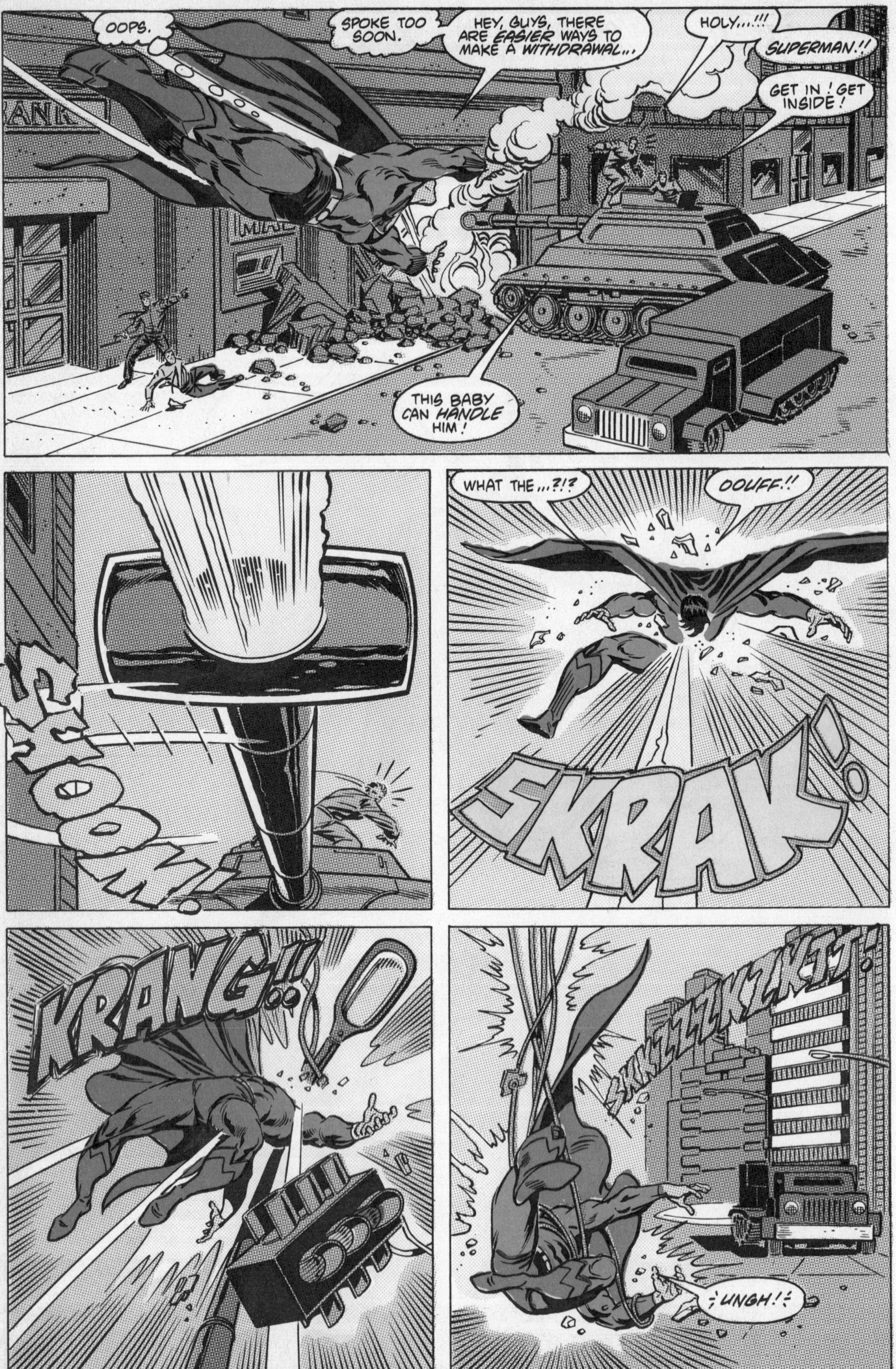
OOPS.
SPOKE TOO SOON.
HEY, GUYS, THERE ARE EASIER WAYS TO MAKE A WITHDRAWAL...
HOLY...!!!
SUPERMAN!!
GET IN! GET INSIDE!
THIS BABY CAN HANDLE HIM!
SHOOM!
WHAT THE...?!?
OOUFF!!
SKRAK!
KRANG!!
UNGH!

NOW... THAT WAS PARTICULARLY... NASTY.

CONCUSSION SHELL... KNOCKED THE WIND OUT OF ME...

AND OUR LITTLE FRIENDS AREN'T ABOUT TO GIVE ME A MOMENT TO RECOVER.

RAM 'IM!!

SQUASH 'IM!!

KRAM!!

UNFORTUNATELY FOR THEM, THEY'RE DOING ME A FAVOR.

NOW THAT I'M OUT OF THAT NEST OF LIVE WIRES...

...I DON'T FEEL LIKE I'VE GOT EVERY SOLDIER ANT IN THE WORLD TRYING TO MAKE A MEAL OUT OF ME.

I CAN CONCENTRATE, AGAIN...

AND I CAN ACT!

SSKRREEKKE

HEY, WHAT GIVES? WE'RE SLOWIN' DOWN!

FLOOR IT, YA DOPE!

WHADDAYA THINK I'M DOIN'?!?

THE WHEELS ARE SPINNIN' AT SEVENTY...

...BUT THEY AIN'T TOUCHIN' TH' GROUND!!

HOLD TIGHT! THE ARMOR PLATING ON THIS HALF-TRACK SHOULD PROTECT YOU FROM...

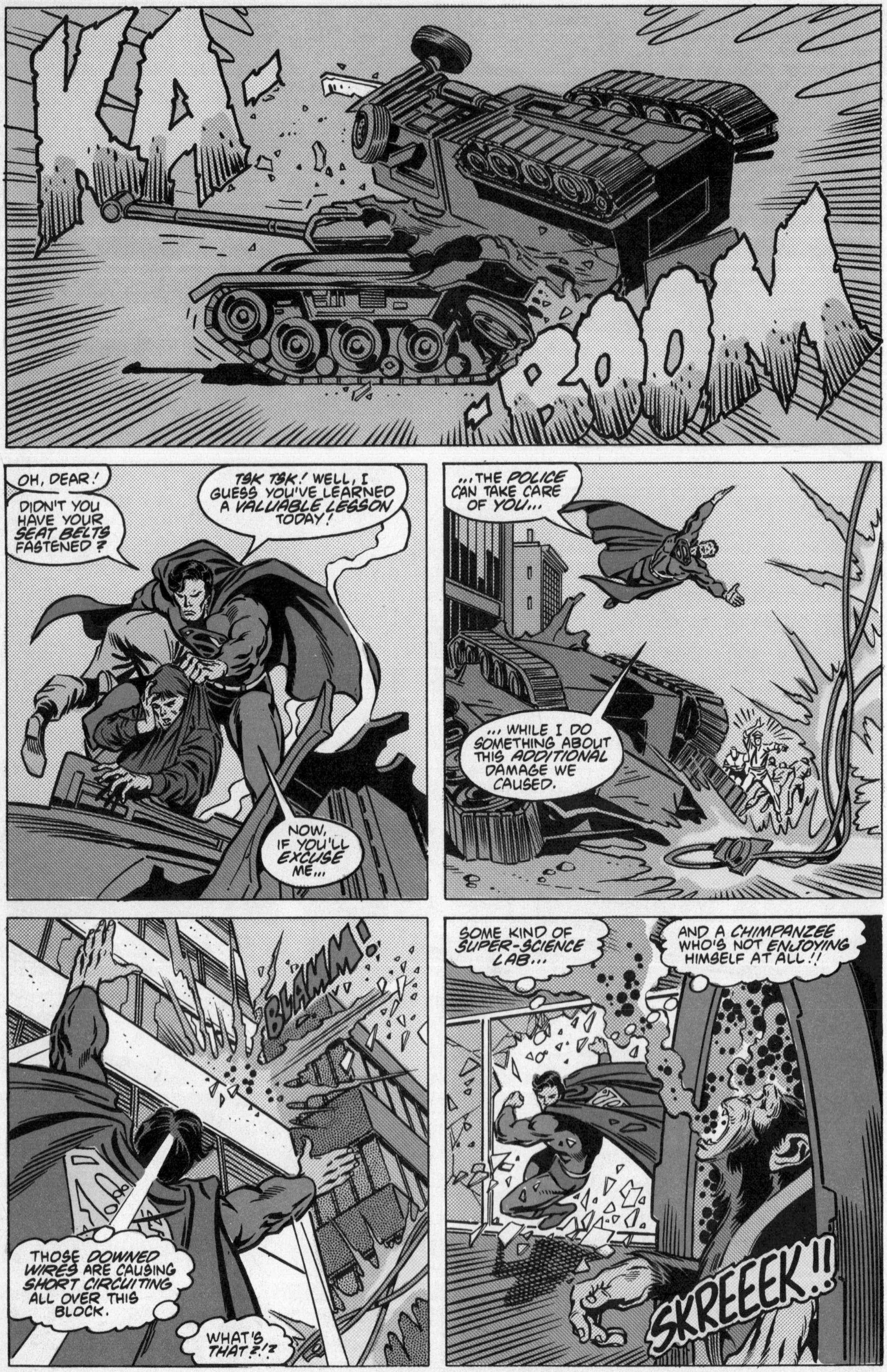
KA-BOOM
OH, DEAR!
DIDN'T YOU HAVE YOUR SEAT BELTS FASTENED?
TSK TSK! WELL, I GUESS YOU'VE LEARNED A VALUABLE LESSON TODAY!
NOW, IF YOU'LL EXCUSE ME...
...THE POLICE CAN TAKE CARE OF YOU...
...WHILE I DO SOMETHING ABOUT THIS ADDITIONAL DAMAGE WE CAUSED.
BLAMM!
THOSE DOWNED WIRES ARE CAUSING SHORT CIRCUITING ALL OVER THIS BLOCK.
WHAT'S THAT?!?
SOME KIND OF SUPER-SCIENCE LAB...
AND A CHIMPANZEE WHO'S NOT ENJOYING HIMSELF AT ALL!!
SKREEEK!!

OBVIOUSLY THE SHORT CIRCUITS HAVE *SCREWED UP* WHATEVER THESE PEOPLE ARE DOING HERE.

THE MAIN FEED'S GONE *WILD!!*

I CAN'T GET NEAR THE CIRCUIT BREAKER!

THOSE MEN DON'T SEEM IN ANY *IMMEDIATE* DANGER.

LET'S TAKE CARE OF OUR FURRY FRIEND FIRST...

EASY, BOY.

IT'S OKAY.

YOU'RE *SAFE* AND...

...*OWWWWWWW!!*

SKREEKTK!!

I... *FELT* THAT!!

HIS TEETH ALMOST *BROKE* THROUGH MY INVULNERABLE *SKIN!*

SUPERMAN!

THE MAIN SWITCH!

YOU *GOTTA PULL* IT!!

EASY ENOUGH, FRIEND.

MY SECOND ELECTRIC *BATH* TODAY.

I WONDER...

COULD THAT *FIRST ZAPPING* HAVE ANYTHING TO DO WITH MY FEELING THAT *BITE?*

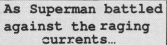

As Superman battled against the raging currents...

I found myself in an **unexpected** battle of my own...

I'M *SORRY,* LOIS.

I KNOW *JUST HOW* YOU FEEL, BELIEVE ME.

BUT THE MOST YOU'VE GOT IS A *HUMAN INTEREST* STORY.

AND THAT'S NOT *PAGE ONE* MATERIAL.

PERRY, YOU'VE GOT TO BE *KIDDING!*

YOU WEREN'T *THERE.* YOU DIDN'T LOOK INTO TITANO'S *EYES.*

YOU DIDN'T SEE THE *FEAR.*

YOU CAN'T TELL ME ANY *SCIENTIFIC* ADVANCE IS *WORTH* THAT KIND OF SUFFERING!

YOU'RE PREACHING TO THE *CONVERTED,* LOIS.

I'M ON *YOUR SIDE.* REALLY.

IN MY LIFE I'VE HAD SIX *DOGS,* EIGHT *CATS*... EVEN A *MONKEY,* ONCE.

NOBODY LOVES ANIMALS MORE THAN I DO. BUT LOVING ANIMALS ISN'T THE *POINT.*

HUMAN *SURVIVAL* IS!

AND DOCTOR *MOYERS* CLAIMS HIS EXPERIMENTS WILL PROVIDE *UNTOLD* BENEFITS FOR HUMANKIND.

AND *THAT'S* YOUR STORY!

ALL RIGHT. HAVE IT *YOUR WAY,* PERRY.

BUT I'M NOT OUT OF *ACES* YET!

NOW WHAT?

YOU... YOU'VE CUT THE *POWER*...

BUT ALL THESE *GASES*... FUMES... COULD BE *DANGEROUS*, SUPERMAN.

GET THAT MAN *OUT* OF HERE.

EVACUATE THE BUILDING.

HURRY, MAN!

I'LL TRY TO *CONTAIN* THE FIRE TO THIS FLOOR.

BLASTED *DISRUPTIONS!*

FIRST THAT *SNOOPING* LANE WOMAN...

I'LL NEVER MEET MY PROMISED SCHEDULE IF WE DON'T...

NOW THIS!

EH? WHAT WAS...

SKREEEEKK!!

NO!!

THUNG!!

THE *SHATTERPROOF* GLASS STOPPED HIM... BUT...

41

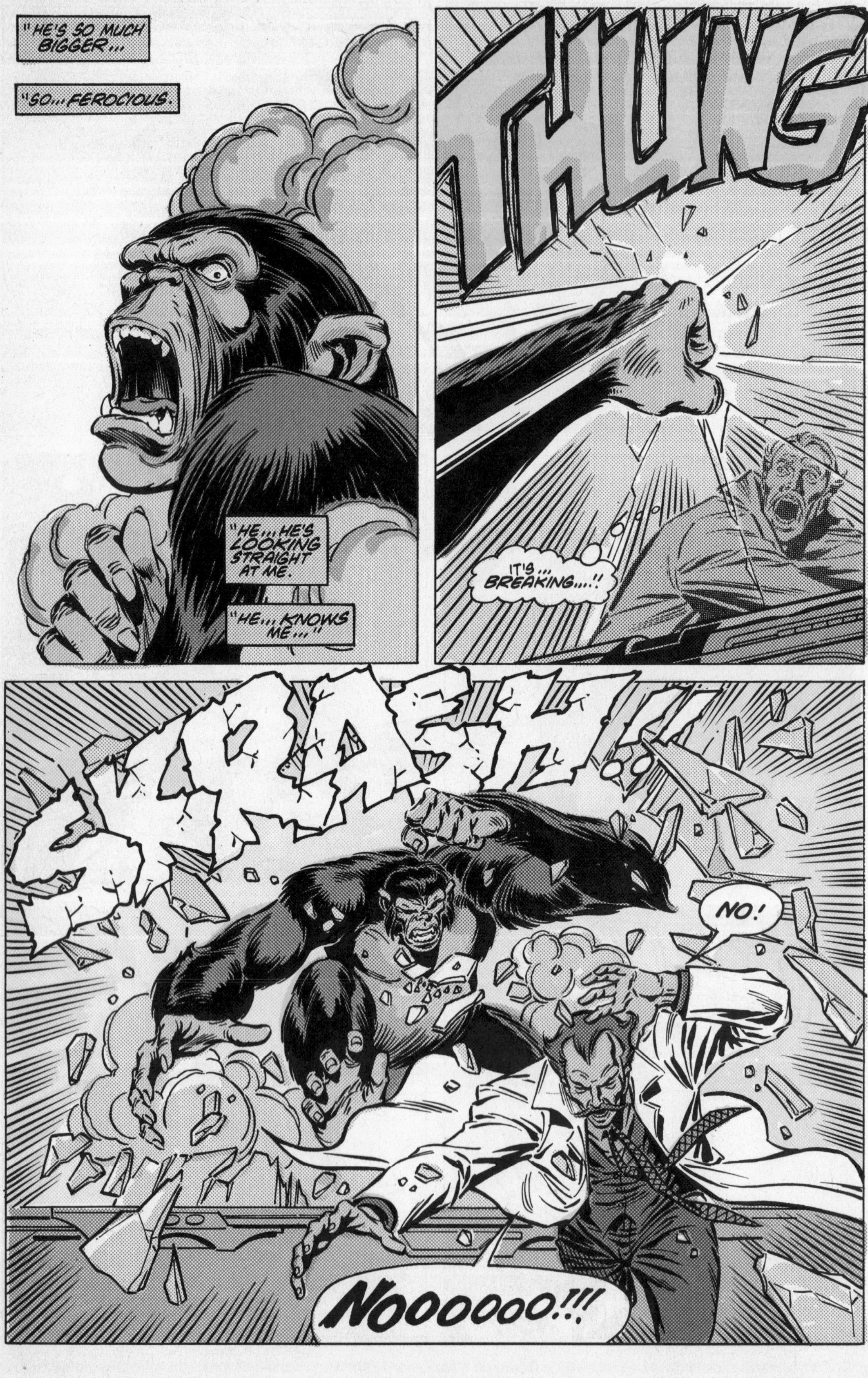
"HE'S SO MUCH BIGGER...
"SO...FEROCIOUS.
"HE...HE'S LOOKING STRAIGHT AT ME.
"HE...KNOWS ME..."
THUNG
IT'S... BREAKING...!!
NO!
NOOOOOO?!!

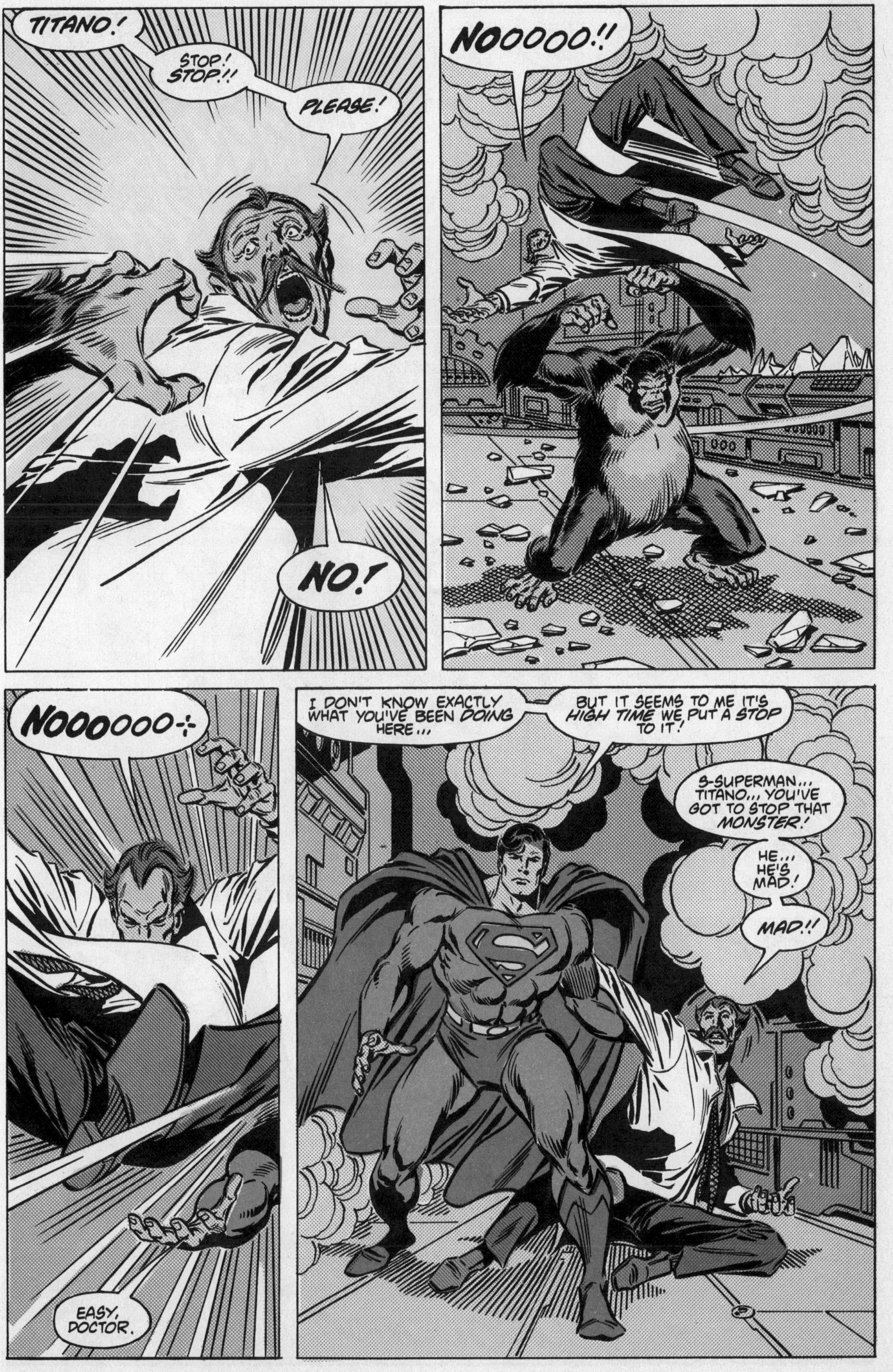
TITANO!
STOP! STOP!!
PLEASE!
NO!
NOOOOO!!
NOOOOOO-!
EASY, DOCTOR.
I DON'T KNOW EXACTLY WHAT YOU'VE BEEN DOING HERE...
BUT IT SEEMS TO ME IT'S HIGH TIME WE PUT A STOP TO IT!
S-SUPERMAN... TITANO... YOU'VE GOT TO STOP THAT MONSTER!
HE... HE'S MAD!
MAD!!

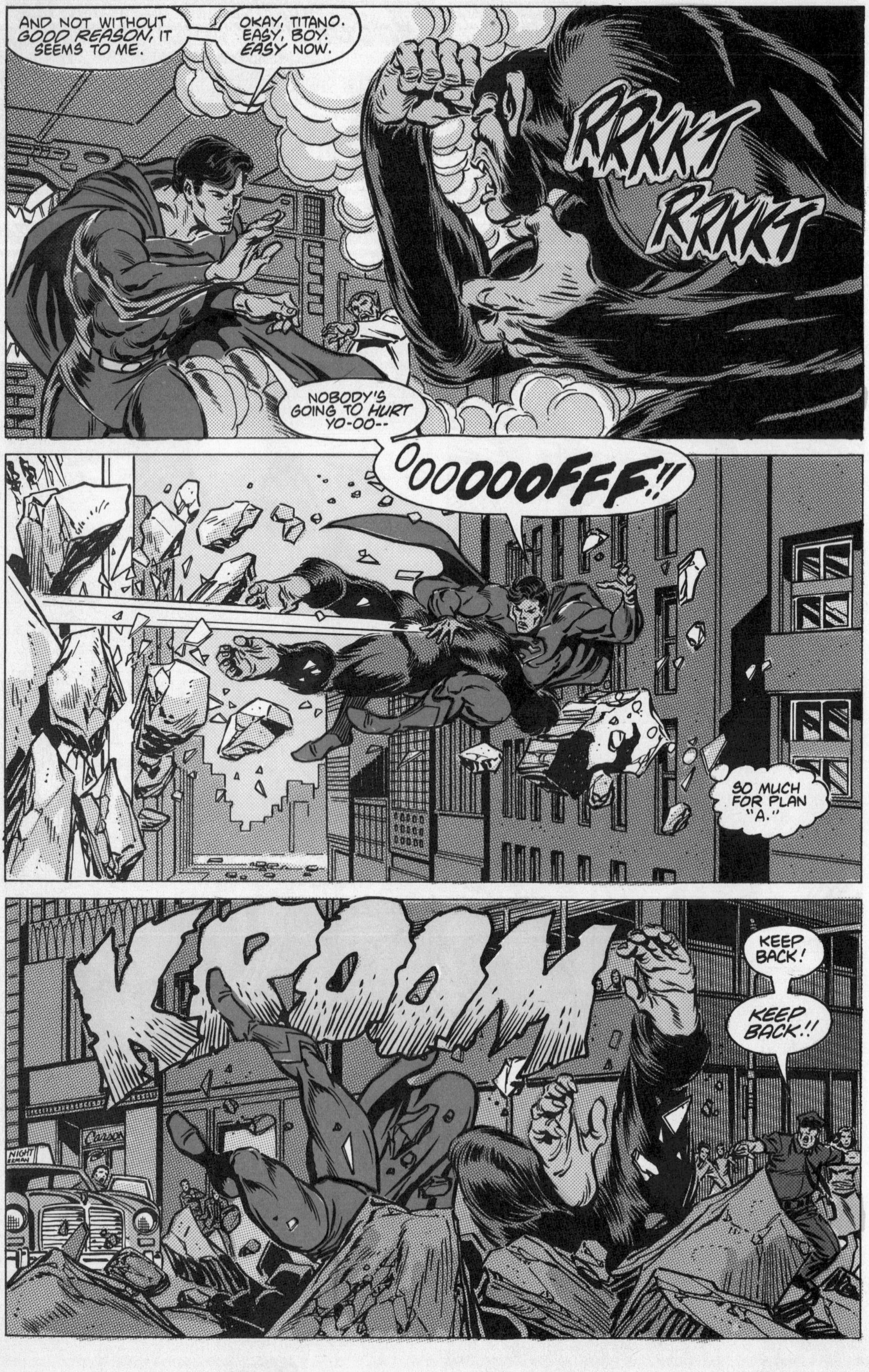
AND NOT WITHOUT GOOD REASON, IT SEEMS TO ME.
OKAY, TITANO. EASY, BOY. EASY NOW.
RRKKT RRKKT
NOBODY'S GOING TO HURT YO-OO--
OOOOOOFFF!!
SO MUCH FOR PLAN "A."
KROOM
KEEP BACK!
KEEP BACK!!

THIS IS REILLY AT 57th AND MONROE!

GET ME CAP'N SAWYER!

THE *IMPACT* SEEMS TO HAVE *SLOWED HIM DOWN* A...

NO...

SPOKE TOO SOON, AGAIN.

HE'S... *GROWING!!*

I'M *SORRY,* MISS LANE...

METROPOLIS HUMANE SOCIETY

WITH THE *CASELOAD* WE HANDLE WE SIMPLY DON'T HAVE *TIME* FOR SOMETHING LIKE THIS.

TITANO'S SITUATION IS *APPALLING*...

BUT IT'S ALSO, SADLY...

QUITE *LEGAL,* I KNOW.

I was beginning to feel positively Quixotic.

I was jousting with windmills...

And the windmills were winning.

...ALL CARS. SUPERMAN IS BATTLING... AND THIS IS NO JOKE, BOYS... A GIANT APE...

"...*APE*..."?

My story had reached Page One...

SKREEECH!!

But, even as I raced across Metropolis...

...Moyers' big mistake was getting even **bigger**...

OH NO!

HE'S EXPERIENCING ANOTHER *GROWTH SURGE!*

WITH THE AMOUNT OF *ENERGY* HE *ABSORBED*...

THERE MAY BE *NO END* TO IT!

THERE IS *ONE WAY* TO END IT, DOCTOR.

IT'S TIME YOU *USED IT!*

BUT... IF I... IF I REPORT A *FAILURE*...

THAT *MONKEY* HAS DEMOLISHED A WHOLE *BLOCK*, DOCTOR.

HE'S NO *SECRET* NOW.

Y-YOU'RE RIGHT, OF COURSE.

I ONLY HOPE....

HELLO...?

THIS IS MOYERS.

CONNECT ME TO *SECTION SEVEN*.

ONE MOMENT, DOCTOR.

SECTION CHIEF *STEEL* COMING ON NOW...

DON'T *TELL* ME, MOYERS. YOU *BLEW IT*, RIGHT?

YOU *ASSURED* ME YOU *KNEW* WHAT YOU WERE *DOING*.

BUT ME NO *BUTS*, MOYERS.

46

"YOUR MISTAKE IS AIRING ALL OVER THE TV.

"WE PAID YOU TO DEVELOP A SUPER-AGENT --

"--NOT TO TURN SOME POOR MONKEY INTO A MONSTER.

"KITTY FAULKNER ALMOST DIED BECAUSE YOU SCREWED UP ONCE BEFORE, MOYERS...*

*IN SUPERMAN #7

"WE BAILED YOU OUT OF THAT ONE BECAUSE YOU PROMISED RESULTS.

"WELL....

"YOUR RESULTS ARE WELL ON THEIR WAY TO DESTROYING METROPOLIS.

"WE'RE GOING TO HAVE TO BAIL YOU OUT AGAIN, AREN'T WE?"

"BUT THIS TIME YOU'RE GONNA BE HELD ACCOUNTABLE!"

MY GOD!

WAS THE BUILDING CLEAR?

FOOM

BRRARRK

OH, NO...

UMPHHH!

I DON'T REALLY *WANT* TO HURT HIM...

BUT HE'S SO *POWERFUL*...

SO *DANGEROUS*...

I MAY NOT BE *ABLE* TO STOP HIM...

"...WITHOUT *KILLING* HIM!"

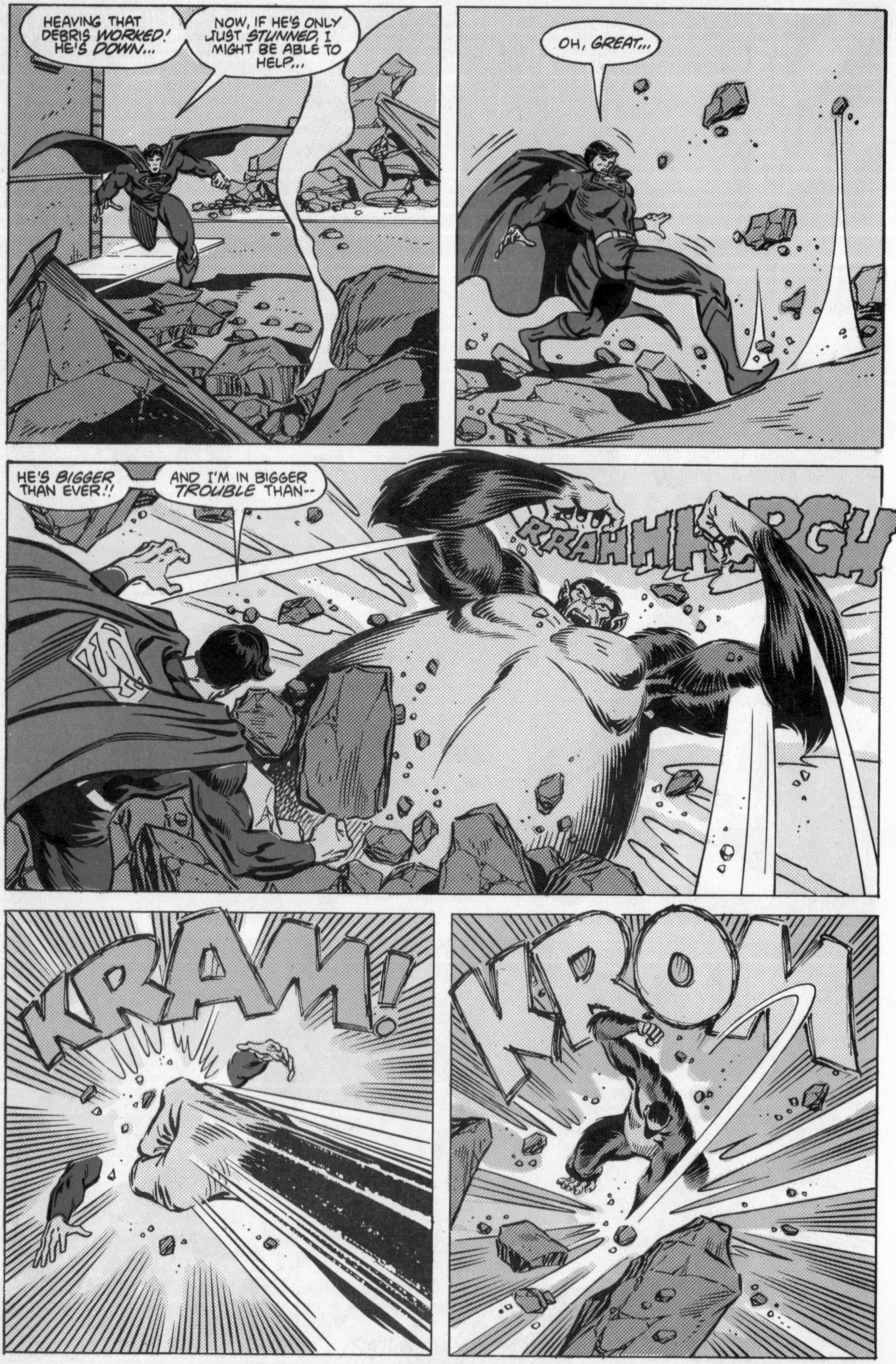
HEAVING THAT DEBRIS WORKED! HE'S DOWN...
NOW, IF HE'S ONLY JUST STUNNED, I MIGHT BE ABLE TO HELP...
OH, GREAT...
HE'S BIGGER THAN EVER!!
AND I'M IN BIGGER TROUBLE THAN--
KRAHHHHRGH
KRAM!
KROW

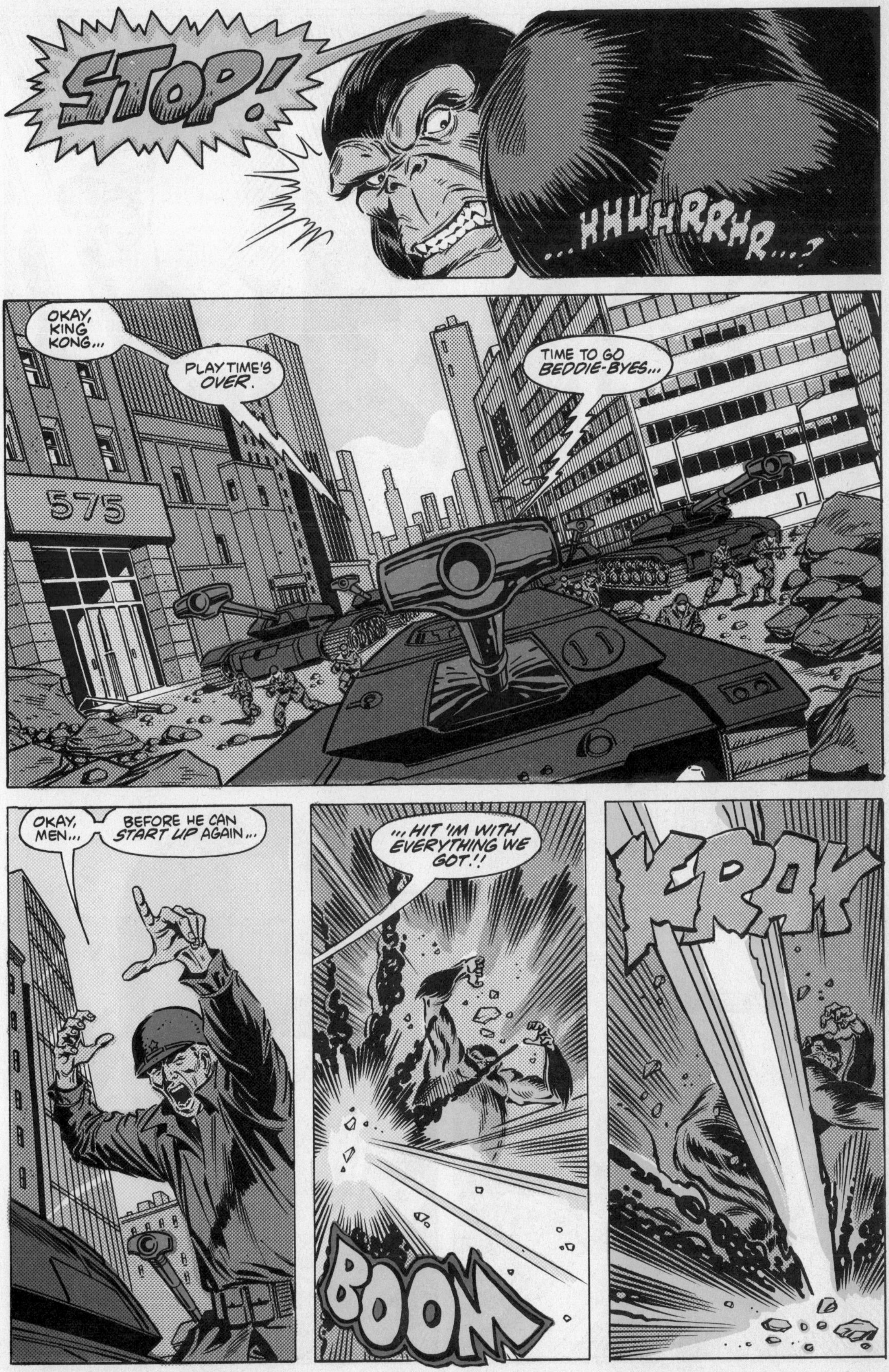
STOP!
...HHUHRRHR...?
OKAY, KING KONG...
PLAYTIME'S OVER.
TIME TO GO BEDDIE-BYES...
575
OKAY, MEN...
BEFORE HE CAN START UP AGAIN...
...HIT 'IM WITH EVERYTHING WE GOT!!
BOOM
KRAK

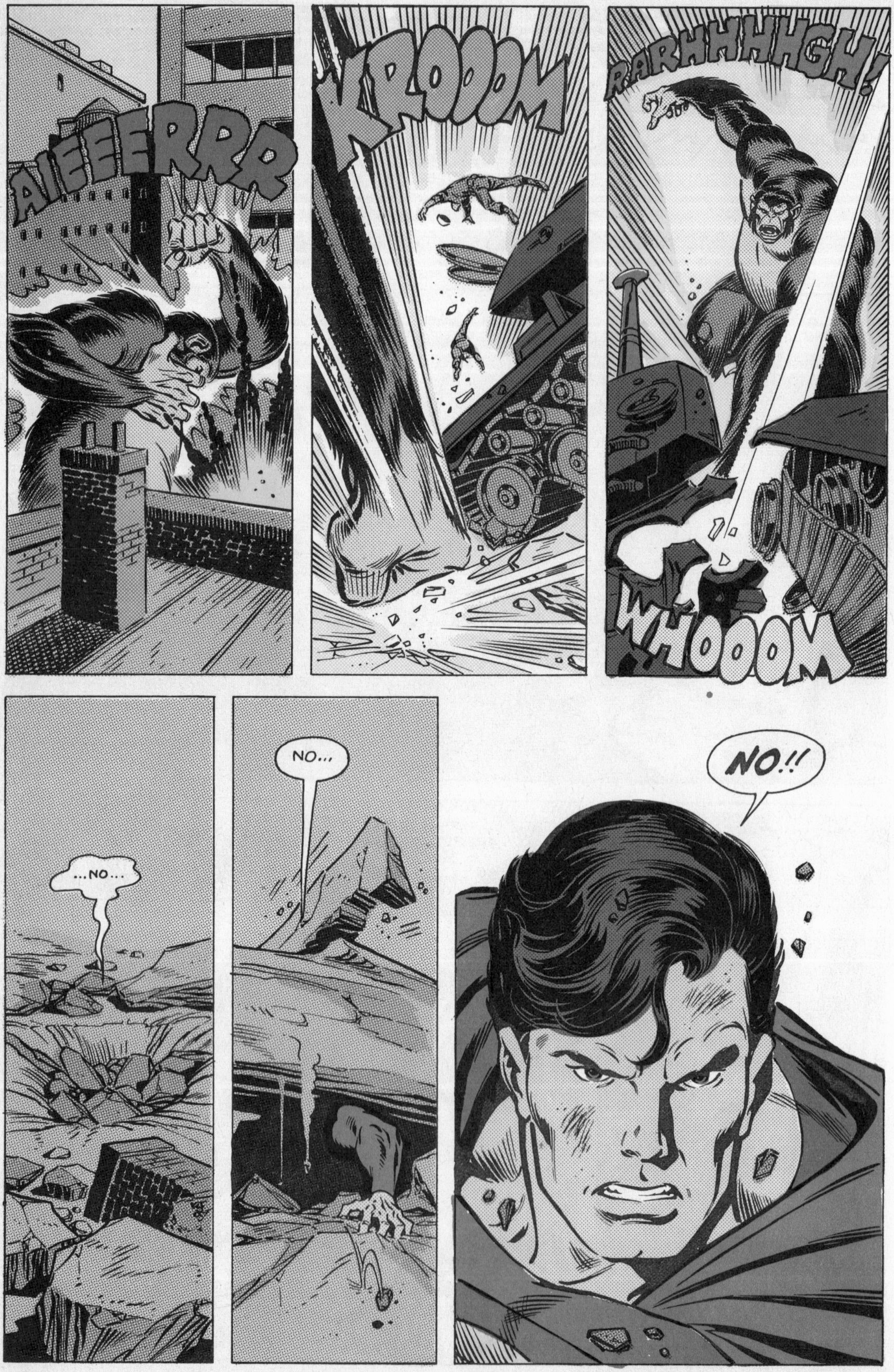
AIEEERRR
KROOOM
RARHHHHGH!
WHOOOM
...NO...
NO...
NO!!

STILL GROGGY... BUT-- THAT 'COPTER...

OBVIOUSLY CO-ORDINATING THE ATTACK.

STOP!!

YOU CAN'T FIGHT TITANO THAT WAY!

MAYBE YOU'VE GOT A BETTER WAY, BIG MAN?

SPARE ME THE SARCASM, COLONEL.

I HAVE A PLAN...

LET ME THROUGH, BLAST YOU, I'M LOIS LANE!

I KNOW WHO YOU ARE, MA'AM. I SEEN YOUR PITCHER IN TH' PLANET.

BUT I GOT EXPRESS ORDERS T'KEEP YOU AWAY FROM HERE...

ORDERS...?

WHO...?

MOYERS! THAT SLIMY LITTLE...

OKAY, COLONEL, ORDER YOUR MEN TO HOLD BACK FOR THREE MINUTES...

...AND I'LL FINISH THIS... THE ONLY WAY POSSIBLE!

AND ONLY PRAY MY CONSCIENCE WILL LET ME LIVE WITH THIS DECISION...

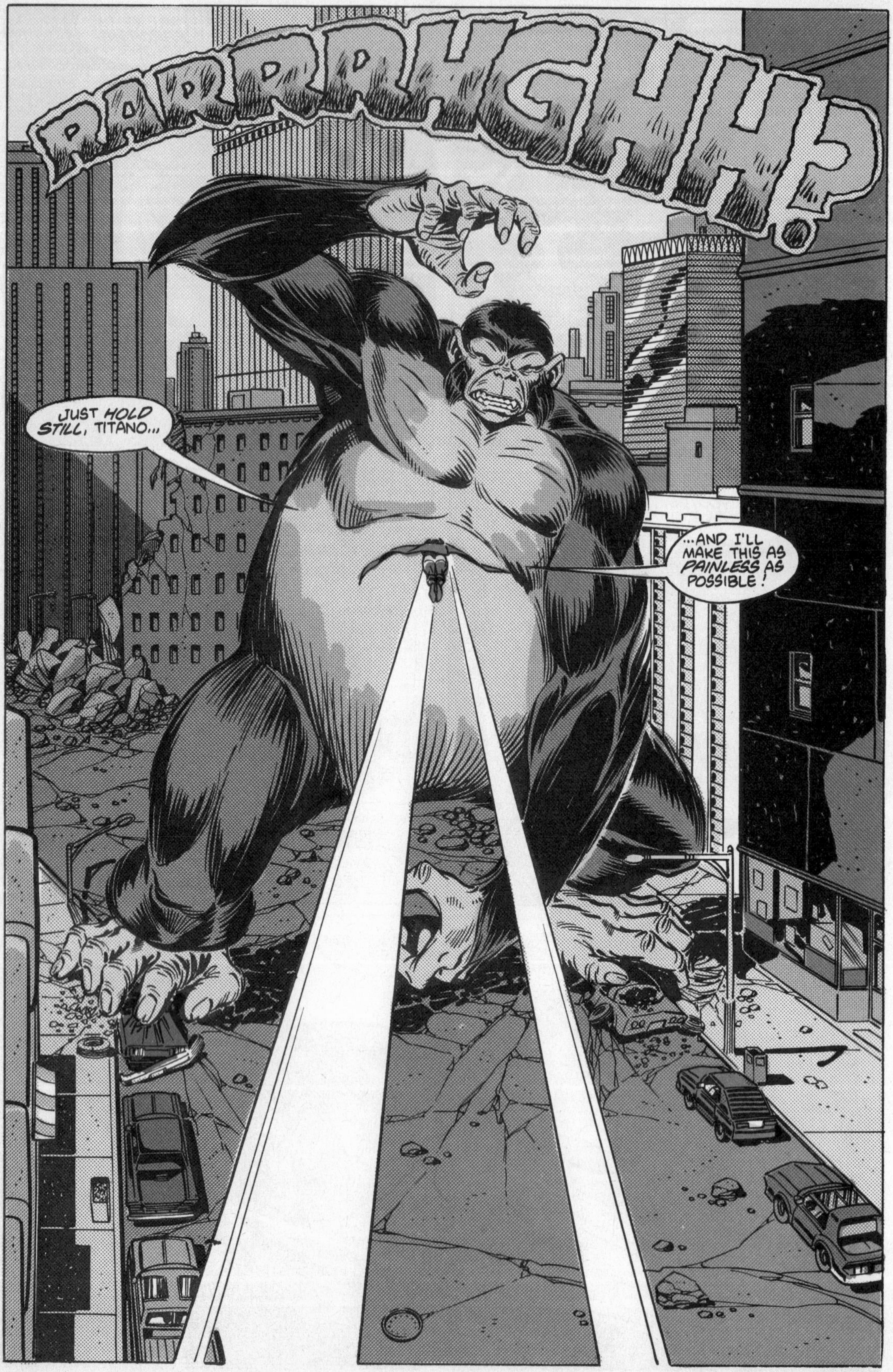
RARRRHGHH!?
JUST HOLD STILL, TITANO...
...AND I'LL MAKE THIS AS PAINLESS AS POSSIBLE!

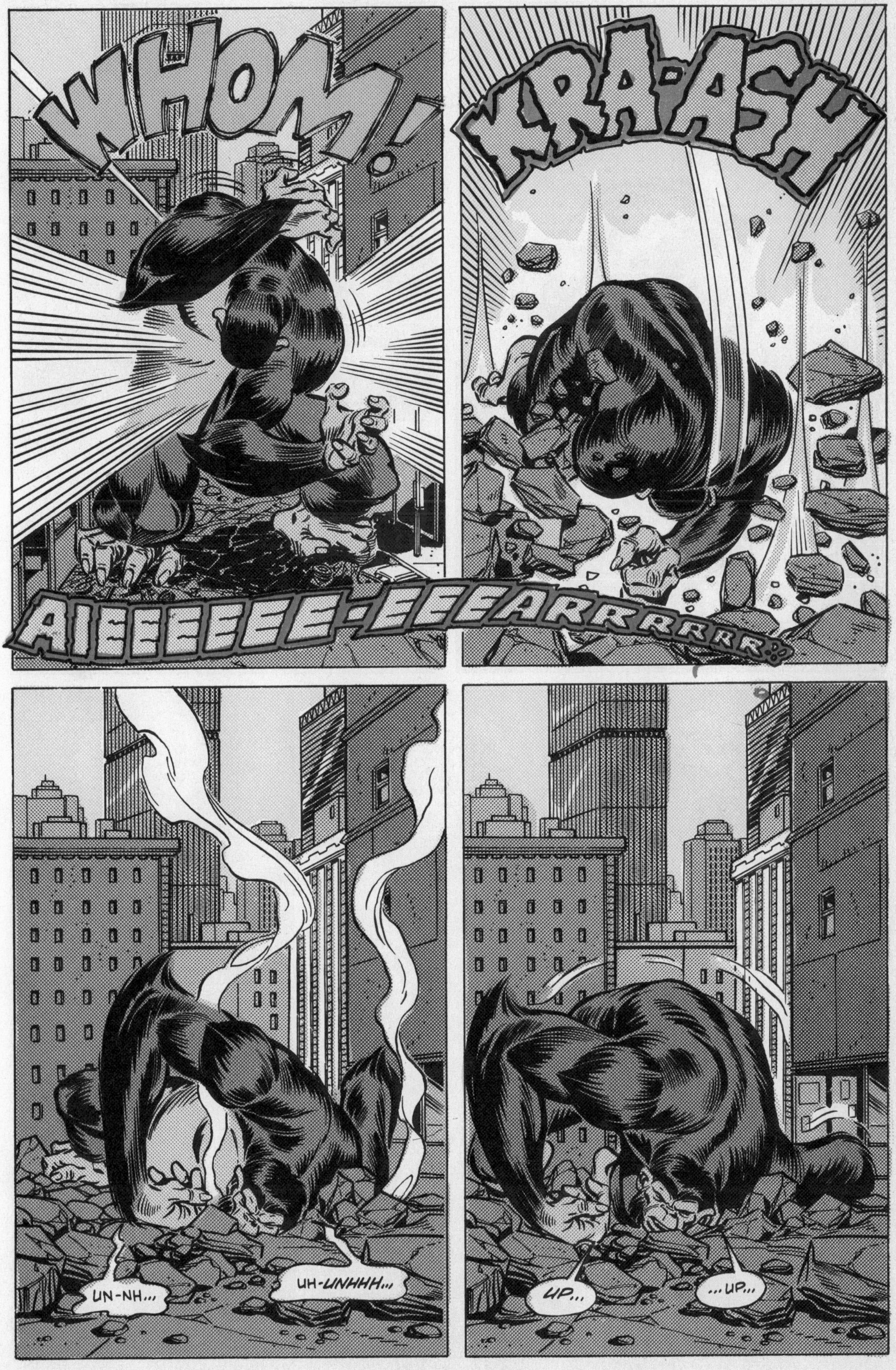
WHOM!
KRA-ASH
AIEEEEEEE-EEEARRRRRRR!
UN-NH...
UH-UNHHH...
UP...
...UP...

...AND AWAY!!!

GOT TO GET HIM *AWAY* FROM THE CITY...

...AWAY FROM *PEOPLE*.

WHAT I'M PLANNING IS GOING TO BE *VERY* DANGEROUS.

IT ALMOST *KILLED* ME WHEN I DID IT TO MYSELF...

BUT,,,

I'VE GOT TO KEEP HIM *DISTRACTED* WHILE I SET THIS UP! FIRST,,,

BOMBS AWAY!

BAFOOSH!

APES *HATE* WATER.

HATE GETTING *WET.*

NOW, WHILE TITANO THRASHES AROUND IN THE EAST RIVER,,,

ZSZKST!!

I'LL JUST *BORROW* A LITTLE *POWER* FROM THIS MAIN GRID CABLE,,,

GOOD, TITANO'S STOPPED THRASHING,,,

AND HE *SEES* THE CABLE,,,

NOW, IF HE'LL JUST,,,

"...GRAB IT..."

YEE·AAHGHHHH!!

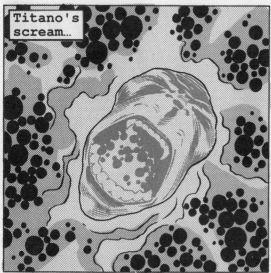

Titano's scream...

There are people in Metropolis -- people ten miles from Metropolis -- who say they'll never forget that sound.

I was eight blocks away.

It cut through my soul like a chainsaw.

I've never driven as fast as I did then.

And still it wasn't fast enough...

T-TITANO...

HE'S... HE'S...

EASY, LOIS.

I PROMISE, HE'S JUST STUNNED.

I TRIED TO USE A MASSIVE CHARGE OF ELECTRICITY TO DRIVE THE RAMPANT ENERGY OUT OF HIM, BUT...

HMM...?

THAT'S ODD...

MY SUPER-HEARING DETECTS A SLOWING OF HIS HEART RATE...

...AT YOUR APPROACH!

HE'S CALMING DOWN!

HE... KNOWS ME.

I WAS THERE...

IN THE LAB...

I TRIED TO PROTECT HIM, SUPERMAN.

HE KNOWS I'M A FRIEND...

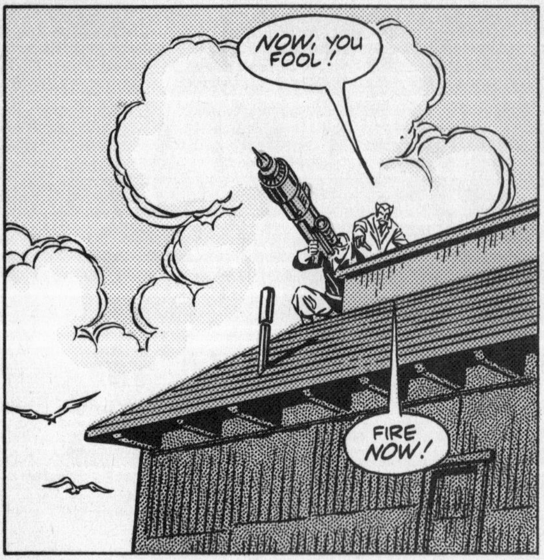
NOW, YOU FOOL!
FIRE NOW!

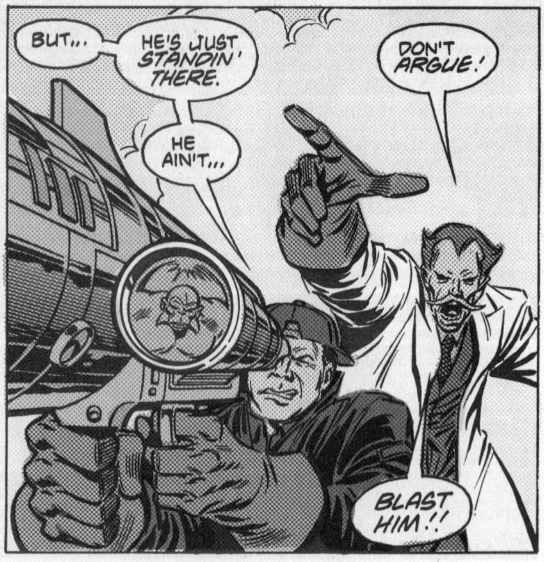
BUT...
HE'S JUST STANDIN' THERE.
HE AIN'T...
DON'T ARGUE!
BLAST HIM!!

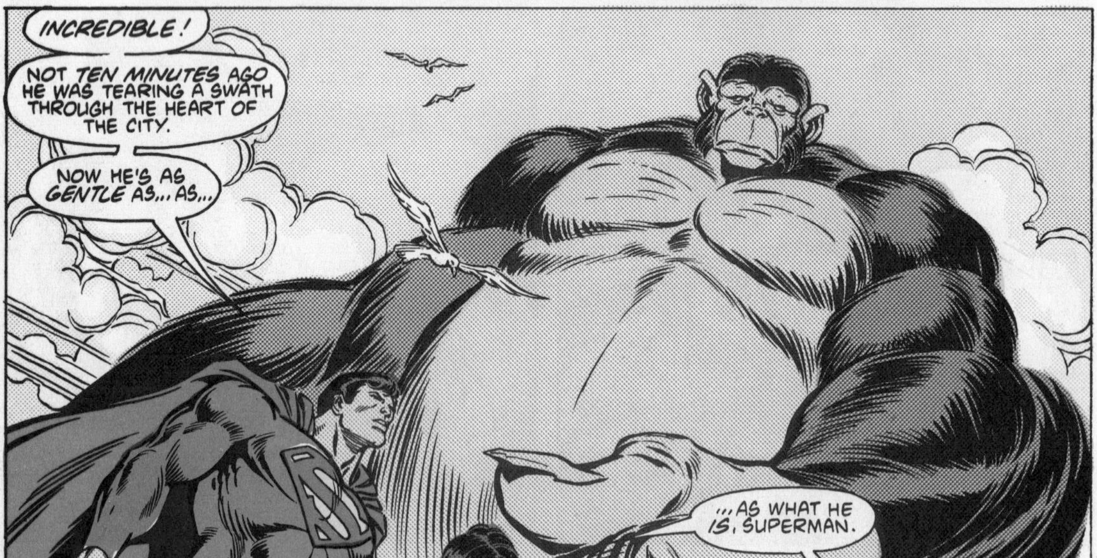
INCREDIBLE!
NOT TEN MINUTES AGO HE WAS TEARING A SWATH THROUGH THE HEART OF THE CITY.
NOW HE'S AS GENTLE AS... AS...
...AS WHAT HE IS, SUPERMAN.
A POOR, FRIGHTENED CHIMP WHO NEVER...

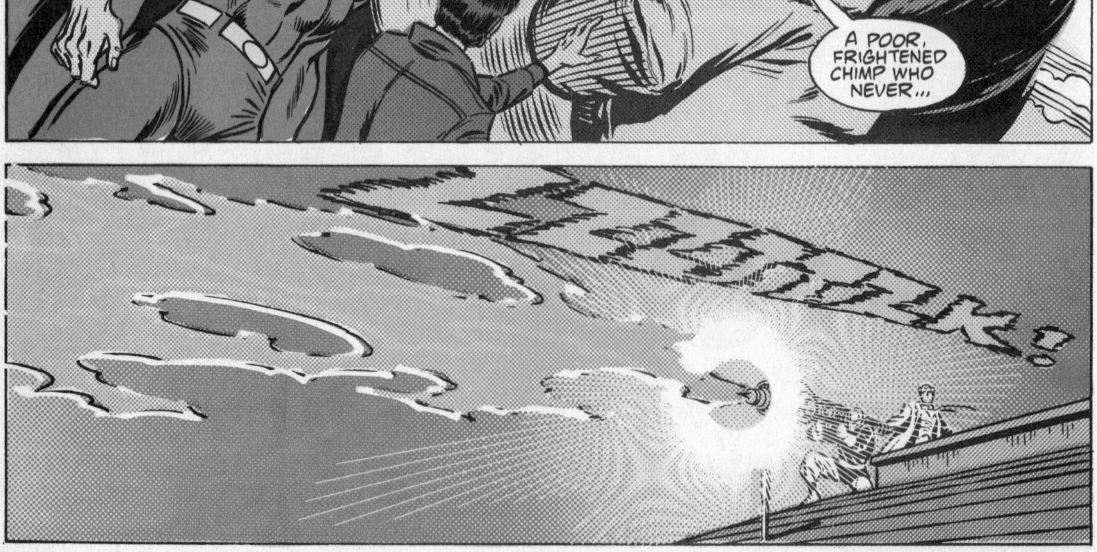

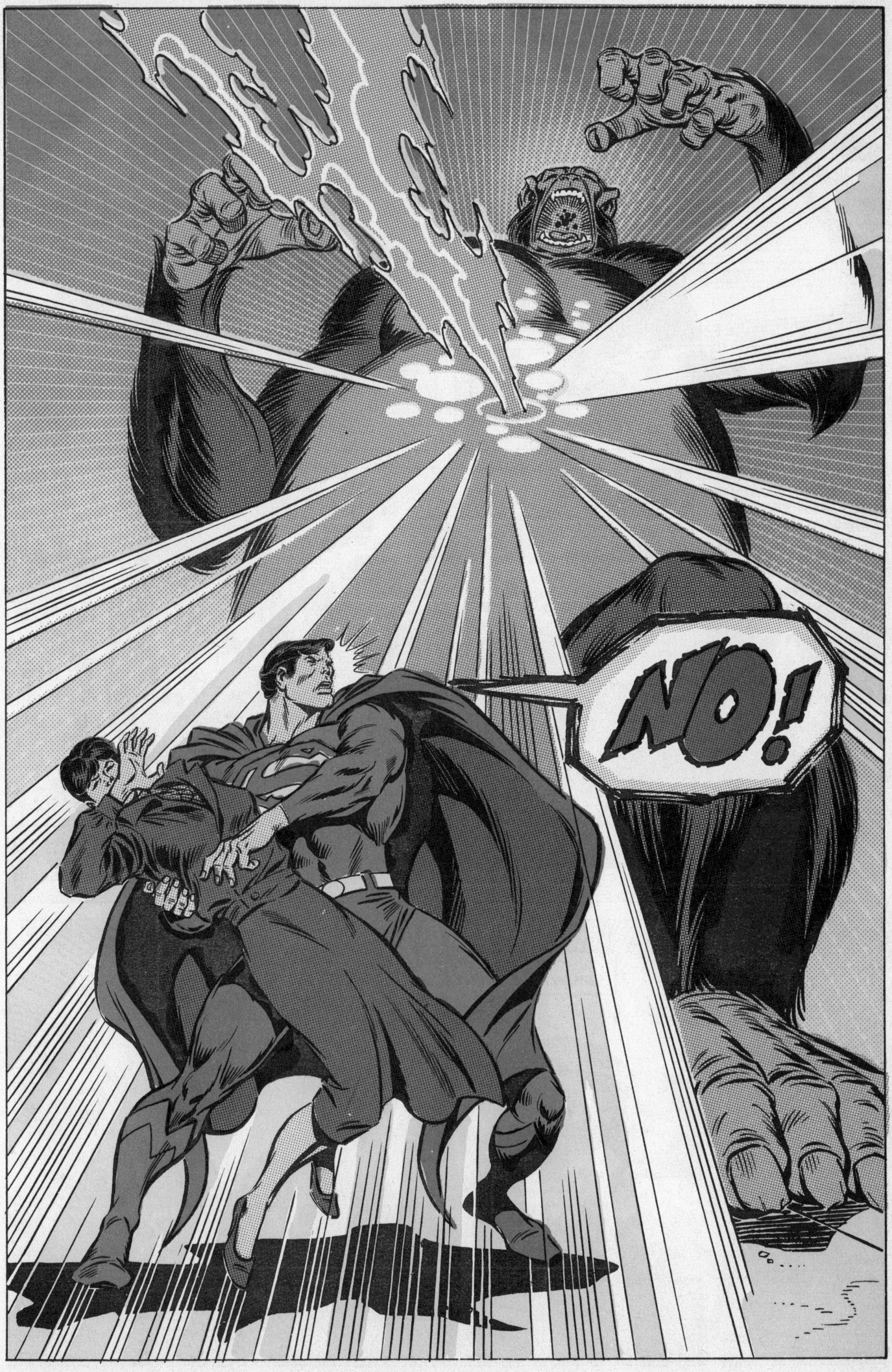
NO!

GREAT SCOTT!

IT'S SOME KIND OF ... FISSION RAY!!

TITANO!

NO!

NO!!

HE'S BURNING!! IT'S AS IF HIS FLESH IS ON FIRE!!

IT IS!

"THAT BOLT THEY HIT HIM WITH SET UP A CHAIN REACTION!

"TITANO'S BODY HAS BECOME AN ATOMIC FURNACE!

"AND HE CAN'T SURVIVE IT!"

KKK-THUMMM

The terrible fury unleashed in his cells accomplished what Superman could not.

The monster dwindled...

Dwindled...

And in its place...

TITANO! HE'S BACK TO NORMAL...

BUT IS HE...?

TITANO...?

SHREEK!

SHREEK!

OH, NO...

...NO...

HE'S AFRAID OF ME!

HE... HE MUST THINK I SET HIM UP...

BETRAYED HIM!

EASY, LOIS. IT'S... NOT YOUR FAULT.

HE...

HE...

EH...?

HOW PATHETIC!

LOOK AROUND YOU, MAN OF STEEL.

LOOK AT THE *DESTRUCTION* THIS BEAST CAUSED WITH ITS *RAMPAGE!*

THEN TELL ME IT *DESERVES* HER TEARS!

"*RAMPAGE*"?

THAT SEEMS A PARTICULARLY *INAPPROPRIATE* CHOICE OF WORDS, MOYERS.

THERE WAS ABSOLUTELY *NO* NEED FOR THIS.

I THINK IT'S TIME SOMEONE TAUGHT YOU SOME *RESPONSIBILITY...*

RES-SPONS...

NOW YOU JUST *WAIT* ONE DAMN MINUTE, *SUPERHERO.*

DON'T YOU *DARE* PREACH AT ME!

EVERY TIME SOME *GOON* COMES TO METROPOLIS, YOU *WRECK* HALF THE CITY FIGHTING HIM.

YOU DID THE SAME *HERE.*

ONLY THIS TIME *I* FINISHED IT!

THE APE WAS *MINE* BY LAW...

...AND I *TOOK* CARE OF IT!

SO HELP ME, MOYERS...

SHUT UP!!

TITANO...?

HE... SAW WHAT YOU DID, LOIS.

HE... UNDERSTANDS NOW.

RIDICULOUS!

HE'S AN ANIMAL!

EEK! EEK!

HE HAS NO FEELINGS! NO COMPREHENSION!

NO?

HE COMPREHENDS PAIN, DOCTOR.

AND I THINK HE COMPREHENDS...

...DEATH...

The other papers told the story of a monster.

A monster that battled Superman.

65

And they were <u>right</u>. There <u>was</u> a monster in Metropolis that day.

An ugly, raging monster, full of death and destruction.

But it did not wear the face of the chimp who died in my arms.

It wore the face it's worn for all the centuries since Cain killed Abel.

The face of a greedy, selfish <u>beast</u>. A beast without equal in the Animal Kingdom.

A beast called <u>Man</u>.

IT'S *HIM*, I TELL YA!

IT'S *REALLY* HIM!

LEX LUTHOR! THE RICHEST MAN IN THE *WORLD!*

SITTIN' THERE EATIN' *STEAK 'N' EGGS!*

AN' HE ASKED FOR *JENNY'S* TABLE!

HER *TIP'S* GONNA PAY OFF HER *MORTGAGE!*

ANYTHING *ELSE* I CAN DO FOR YOU, SIR?

YES...

YOU CAN *JOIN* ME FOR A LITTLE WHILE.

?

OH... ER... NO, SIR! I *COULDN'T* DO *THAT!*

I... I'M VERY *FLATTERED,* MR. LUTHOR...

BUT RALLI'S *COMPANY POLICY* SAYS WE CAN'T SIT WITH THE *CUSTOMERS.*

NOT WHILE WE'RE ON *DUTY,* ANYWAYS.

JENNY

RALLI'S COMPANY POLICY IS OF *SMALL INTEREST* TO ME, MY DEAR.

IF YOU'VE GUESSED WHO I *AM,* YOU SHOULD ALSO BE ABLE TO GUESS THAT I PROBABLY *OWN* THIS RESTAURANT.

AFTER ALL, I OWN *NINETY PERCENT* OF THE *STATE.*

NOW, PLEASE...

SIT.

ER... WELL...

MAYBE... FOR A *MINUTE* I COULD JUST...

2

A *MINUTE?* NO, NO, MY DEAR.

I WAS THINKING MORE ALONG THE ORDER OF A *MONTH.*

WH... *WHAT??*

I *NOTICED* YOU WHEN I FIRST CAME IN... *JENNY,* IS IT?

I ASKED FOR ONE OF YOUR TABLES, SPECIFICALLY.

NOW, I'M INVITING YOU TO COME *WITH* ME.

COME BACK WITH ME TO *METROPOLIS.*

FOR *ONE MONTH.*

M-MR. LUTHOR! I...I HAPPEN TO BE *MARRIED!*

AND... AND EVEN IF I *WASN'T...*

I'M...WELL, I'M *NOT THAT KIND OF GIRL!*

OH, *TOSH,* JENNY! IF I'VE LEARNED *NOTHING ELSE* FROM MY *EIGHT* WIVES...

IT IS THAT *EVERYONE* IS *"THAT KIND OF GIRL."*

IT'S ONLY A MATTER OF *PRICE.*

FOR SOME IT'S A *WEDDING RING.*

FOR SOME A *HOLLYWOOD CONTRACT.*

I'M PREPARED TO OFFER YOU...

OH, LET'S MAKE IT... *ONE MILLION DOLLARS,* SHALL WE?

ONE MILLION DOLLARS IN EXCHANGE FOR *ONE MONTH* OF YOUR LIFE.

FAIR?

M-MISTER LUTHOR...!!

Y-YOU MAY BE THE RICHEST MAN IN THE WORLD...

YOU MAY BE *USED* TO GETTING YOUR OWN WAY ON EVERYTHING...

BUT IF YOU THINK YOU CAN JUST COME *WALTZING* IN HERE AND...

3

CALM YOUR-SELF.

YOU'RE REACTING *EMOTIONALLY*, NOT *LOGICALLY*.

I DO NOT MAKE THIS OFFER *LIGHTLY*, JENNY.

LOOK AROUND YOU. YOUR *JOB*. YOUR *PLACE* IN THE WORLD.

SHALL I TELL YOU THE *STORY* OF YOUR LIFE, JENNY?

PAST, PRESENT... AND FUTURE?

YOU WERE *BORN* HERE, WEREN'T YOU? NOT MORE THAN A *MILE* FROM THIS SPOT.

YOU GREW IN THE SHADOW OF THAT *SIGN* OUT THERE ON THE HIGHWAY.

METROPOLIS 900 Mi

THE ONE THAT SAYS "METROPOLIS-- *900 MILES*."

YOU WERE A BRIGHT CHILD. EVEN *PRECOCIOUS*. YOU *SANG* ALL THE TIME.

IN GRADE SCHOOL YOU *DANCED* IN THE SCHOOL PLAY.

YOU WERE... A *SUNFLOWER*?

...A BUTTERFLY...

A BUTTERFLY. OF COURSE.

HIGH SCHOOL CHEERLEADER? MOST POPULAR GIRL IN THE SCHOOL?

DATED THE FOOT-BALL HERO. MARRIED HIM.

NO FURTHER EDUCATION FOR EITHER OF YOU, AFTER THAT. COULDN'T *AFFORD* IT.

AND NOW YOU'RE... TWENTY-TWO?

WITH A *HUSBAND*, AND A *HOUSE*, AND A *MORTGAGE*.

AND SOMEDAY THREE OR FOUR *CHILDREN*.

A *TELEVISION SET* TO SHOW YOU THE WORLD. A *HIGHWAY SIGN* TO REMIND YOU OF YOUR *DREAMS*.

NINE HUNDRED MILES TO METROPOLIS, JENNY.

NINE HUNDRED MILES TO *TOMORROW*.

A MILLION DOLLARS CAN BUY A *LOT* OF TOMORROWS, JENNY.

IT CAN BUY A *MILLION* TOMORROWS.

AND ALL IT WILL *COST* YOU IS ONE MONTH.

THINK ABOUT IT, JENNY.

I'M GOING TO WAIT IN MY CAR.

FOR *EXACTLY* TEN MINUTES, JENNY.

THINK.

4

GOOD DAY TO YOU, LADIES.

JENNY! WHAT IN HECK WAS THAT ALL ABOUT??

WHEN YOU STARTED IN T' SHOUTIN' AT HIM I THOUGHT I'D HAVE KITTENS!

HE...HE OFFERED ME A MILLION DOLLARS TO GO TO METROPOLIS WITH HIM.

TO BE HIS... I... I CAN'T EVEN SAY IT... FOR A MONTH.

HE'S... WAITING IN HIS CAR FOR MY ANSWER.

SHEEE-OOOT!! YOU'RE KIDDING!!

YOU GONNA DO IT, JEN?

WIH-WHAT?!? SEZ YOU, HONEY!

ASSIE-- Y-YOU'RE NOT... SERIOUS.?!?

BOY! IF SOMEBODY'D OFFERED ME A MILLION BUCKS TO BLOW THIS TOWN WHEN I WAS YOUR AGE...!!

ASSIE!! I CAN'T BELIEVE YOU MEAN THAT! FOR GOD'S SAKE-- HE WANTS ME TO...

...TO...

TO WHAT? TO HAVE THE TIME OF YOUR LIFE FOR A MONTH?

AN' COME BACK WITH ENOUGH MONEY THAT YOU 'N' WALLY WOULD BE SET FOREVER?

HONEY, IF I WAS YOU I'D SURE THINK ABOUT IT.

I'D THINK ABOUT IT REAL HARD!

5

WH-WHAT ARE YOU GONNA *DO*, JENNY?

ARE YOU GONNA...

Y'KNOW...

GONNA...

OH, FOR *PETE'S* SAKE!! WHAT'S WRONG WITH EVERYBODY ALL OF A SUDDEN?

PAM! DON'T TELL ME *YOU* THINK I SHOULD GO?

NO! I MEAN...

I DON'T *THINK* SO. I MEAN...

JEEZ, JENNY! NOBODY'S *EVER* GONNA MAKE *ME* AN OFFER LIKE *THAT!*

BUT *YOU*... YOU WERE ALWAYS THE MOST POPULAR GIRL IN SCHOOL...

OHH... DON'T *YOU* SAY THAT, PAM! THAT'S JUST WHAT *HE* SAID!

HE...HE SAT THERE AND TOLD ME THE STORY OF MY *WHOLE LIFE!*

AND HE MADE IT SOUND SO *STUPID*, AND *SENSELESS*, AND... AND *BORING!*

A... *MILLION* DOLLARS IS SURE A LOTTA *MONEY*, JEN.

YOU COULD PAY OFF YOUR *HOUSE*... GET A NEW *CAR*...

DUMP THAT *JERK* YOU MARRIED...

NO! NO! I DIDN'T *SAY* THAT! *I DIDN'T* SAY THAT!

I'M.... *SORRY*, JENNY. I'M JUST BEING NO HELP AT ALL!

HELLO, *CARTER'S* GAS STATION?

IS *WALLY HUBBARD* THERE?

THANKS...

HIYA... *WALLY* TH' *WIZ* HERE...

HELLO...?

6

72

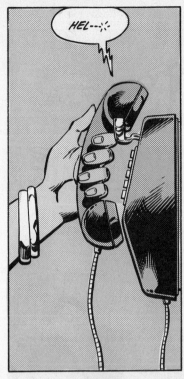

HEL---✶

JENNY...

HE...

HE'S GONE...

YOU WAITED A LOT *LONGER* THAN *USUAL,* BOSS.

ALMOST THE *WHOLE* TEN MINUTES!

THIS ONE NEEDED THE EXTRA *FINESSE,* CYNTHIA.

THE EXTRA *TANTALIZATION.*

SHE SEEMED OF SOMEWHAT *STRONGER MORAL FIBRE* THAN SOME OF THE *OTHERS* WITH WHOM WE'VE PLAYED THIS LITTLE *GAME* IN THE PAST.

BUT THE *RESULT* IS THE *SAME.*

JENNY HUBBARD WILL *NEVER KNOW* WHAT HER FINAL CHOICE WOULD HAVE BEEN.

AND THAT *QUESTION* WILL *TORMENT* HER FOR THE REST OF HER *MEANINGLESS* LIFE!

NOW...HOME TO METROPOLIS, CYNTHIA.

BACK TO *PROJECT OVERLOAD!*

YESSIR!!

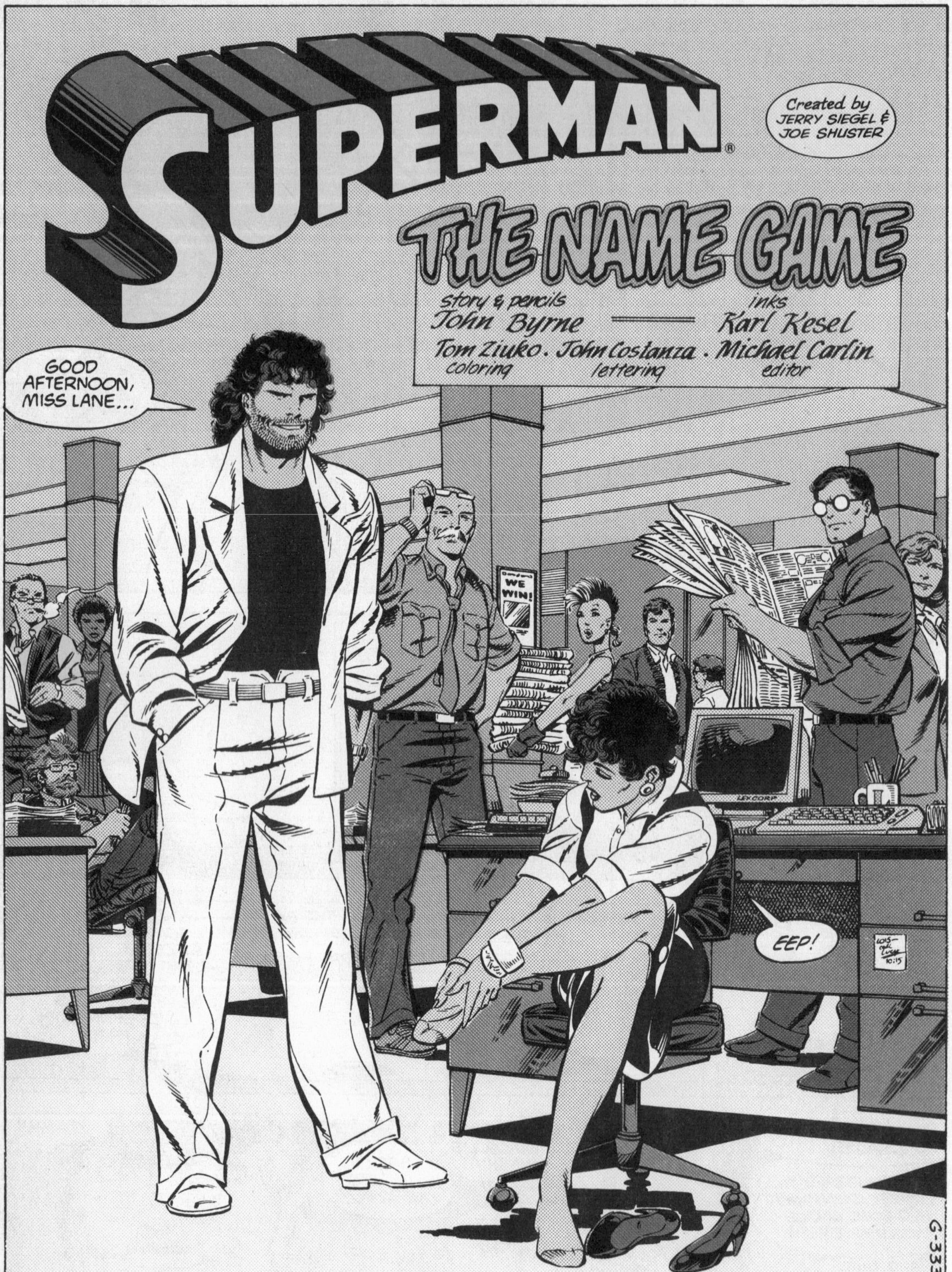
SUPERMAN®
Created by JERRY SIEGEL & JOE SHUSTER
THE NAME GAME
story & pencils John Byrne — inks Karl Kesel
Tom Ziuko . John Costanza . Michael Carlin
coloring lettering editor
GOOD AFTERNOON, MISS LANE...
WE WIN!
LEXCORP
EEP!
G-3336

TIRED FEET?

ALLOW *ME*, MISS LANE.

HEY, WAIT! I DON'T EVEN KNO-O-O-OOOHHHHH!

YOU... DO... THAT... *VERY WELL*, MISTER...

MISTER...?

I DON'T BELIEVE I *CAUGHT* THE NAME...?

I DON'T BELIEVE I *THREW* IT.

DeROY IS THE NAME, MISS LANE. *BEN DeROY.*

I'VE COME TO TAKE YOU OUT TO *LUNCH.*

LUNCH...?

OH, BUT I...

LOIS...

YOU *HAVE* A LUNCH DATE TODAY.

WITH *ME!*

I HADN'T *FORGOTTEN*, CLARK.

I WAS JUST ABOUT TO *TELL* MR. DeROY...

...THAT I'D BE ABSOLUTELY *DELIGHTED* TO HAVE LUNCH WITH HIM!

2

75

WHAT IN THE...??

DON'T LET HER GET YOU *DOWN*, CLARKIE.

C'MON. NO POINT *WASTING* A LOVELY AFTERNOON.

I'LL BUY *YOU* LUNCH!

OH--ER--*CAT!*

ER--YES. THANKS, THANKS VERY MUCH.

THAT... DIDN'T SEEM *AT ALL* LIKE THE LOIS I KNOW.

"WHAT COULD'VE GOTTEN *INTO* HER?"

DID YOU *ENJOY* THAT, MISS *LANE?*

IT WAS FRANKLY *FABULOUS*, MR. DeROY.

EXCEPT...

EXCUSE ME. THIS HAPPENS TO BE THE *NO SMOKING* SECTION, FELLA.

SO? THIS ALSO HAPPENS TO BE A *FREE COUNTRY*, MISS BUTT-IN-SKI!

I'LL SMOKE ANYWHERE I DAMN WELL *PLEASE!*

AND IF YOU DON'T *LIKE* IT, YOU CAN...

... MOVE...!!!

IT'S NEARLY *FOUR*, MISS LANE. I SUPPOSE I SHOULD GET YOU BACK TO THE *OFFICE*.

ER...YES. I SUPPOSE SO!

ODD... EVEN WITH THE *WINDOWS* OPEN IT'S BECOME SUDDENLY *HOT* IN HERE!

MY HAND!

AHHGH!!

AHHGH!!!

MY HAND!!!

IT'S *FORTY* BLOCKS TO THE *DAILY PLANET* BUILDING.

SHALL I HAIL A TAXI?

NO.

IT'S SUCH A *BEAUTIFUL* AFTERNOON I FEEL LIKE *WALKING*.

FUNNY. ONLY A FEW HOURS AGO MY FEET WERE *KILLING* ME.

NOW I FEEL AS IF I'M *WALKING* ON AIR!

YES...

AS YOU SAY...

FUNNY...

MIKEY!!

WILL YOU *PLEASE* PICK THAT THING *UP!!*

NO! NO! GOR-KA WANNA WALK!

GOR-KA WANNA WALK!!

I'M *NOT* BEING A VERY GOOD *REPORTER*.

OOKA-OOKA-OOKA-AAPPP

FOUR HOURS I'VE BEEN WITH YOU, AND I DON'T EVEN KNOW WHERE YOU'RE *FROM!*

OH...*HERE* AND *THERE*.

YONDER, LET'S SAY, YES...

YONDER...

4

"YONDER"? YES ..YES, I SUPPOSE THAT WILL DO.

IT HAS JUST THE RIGHT TOUCH OF MYSTERY... OF ROMANCE...

MIKEY!!

OH, GOD, NO!!

NOOOOO!

ROMANCE...

AH, YES. I'M SO GLAD YOU BROUGHT THAT UP, MISS LANE...

YOU SEE... THERE'S SOMETHING I WANT TO ASK YOU...

MEANWHILE...

I TELL YA, MR. OLSEN, IT WAS THE CRAZIEST THING I EVER SEEN!

AND THIS WAS JUST THIS MORNING, YOU SAID? RIGHT AFTER YOU OPENED?

YEP. WE ALREADY HAD A PRETTY FULL STORE, WHAT WITH THIS BEING TH' FIRST DAY OF OUR BIG WHITE SALE.

WHEN ALL OF A SUDDEN...

"WELL... JUST LIKE *THAT* TH' WHOLE *STORE* WENT CRAZY!

"THERE WAS *SHEETS* AN' *LINEN* AN' *TOWELS* FLYING EVERY WHICH WAY!"

"AN' RIGHT IN THE *MIDDLE* OF IT ALL..."

WELL, THAT WAS *STIMULATING*...

BUT I REALLY CAME HERE FOR A MUCH *BIGGER* GAME.

GOOD MORNING, LADIES!!

HUH! SURE SOUNDS LIKE THERE WAS A LOT *MORE* TO THIS THAN JUST SOME *PUBLICITY STUNT* FOR A WHITE SALE.

TIME TO CALL OUT THE *BIG GUNS*, I'D SAY.

ZEEEEE ZEE EEE

THAT'S WHAT I WAS *HOPIN'* YOU'D DO WHEN I CALLED TH' *DAILY PLANET!*

STILL WAITING FOR LOIS TO COME BACK FROM LUNCH, CLARKIE?

PUT HER OUT OF YOUR MIND, WHY DON'T YOU?

LET ME COME UP TO YOUR APART- MENT THIS EVENING AND I'LL BAKE YOU UP SOME OF MY *WORLD CLASS* LASAGNA.

WELL... THAT *DOES* SOUND *TEMPTING*, CAT...

BUT I'M QUITE *WORRIED* ABOUT LOIS. TO HAVE ACTED SO *STRANGELY*...

AND THEN TO BE *GONE* ALL AFTERNOON...

I REALLY THINK I SHOULD...

UH-OH... JIMMY'S *SIGNAL WATCH!*

CLARK!

SORRY, CAT.

HAVE TO TAKE A *RAIN CHECK* ON THAT LASAGNA.

SOMETHING... JUST CAME UP.

SOMETHING THAT MAY BE A *JOB*...

FOR SUPERMAN!

NOW... WHERE'S JIMMY? THE HYPERSONIC SIGNAL IS COMING FROM THE NORTH-WEST.

A QUICK SCAN WITH MY TELESCOPIC VISION SHOULD...

GREAT SCOTT!!

THAT'S NOT WHAT JIMMY'S SIGNALLING ME ABOUT...

BUT IT'S SOMETHING I'VE GOT TO TAKE CARE OF.

AND NOW!!

THUMP THUMP 'N THUMP

OKAY, BIG BOY, PLAYTIME'S OVER!

LET'S SEE IF WE CAN'T FIND OUT WHERE YOU ESCAPED FROM.

PRESUMABLY A CIRCUS, SINCE ZOOS DON'T GENERALLY DYE THEIR ANIMALS.

7

POING!

?!?

KRAK

WHAT IN THE NAME OF...??

THIS WAS A *LIVING,* *BREATHING,* FULL-SIZED GORILLA!

I *TOUCHED* IT!

SMELLED IT!

WHAAAH!!

HE *BROKE* GOR-KA! HE *BROKE* GOR-KA!!

SH-SHUT *UP,* MIKEY!!

MA'M...

THIS *TOY*... IT *BELONGS* TO YOU?

WHAT HAPPENED HERE?

I...I...I DON'T *KNOW,* SUPERMAN. WE...WE WERE JUST *WALKING*...IT WAS RAINING...

I REMEMBER...WE'D JUST *PASSED* THIS GUY... THIS *GREAT* BIG GUY IN A *WHITE SUIT*...

AND... HE WAS WITH A WOMAN WHO LOOKED LIKE...

"*LOIS* LANE..."

M-MARRY YOU??

BUT... MR. DEROY, WE HARDLY... ...KNOW... OH, YES! YES!!

OH, MR. DEROY, YOU'VE MADE ME THE HAPPIEST WOMAN...

SAY... HOLD ON A MINUTE!

WHERE HAS MY MIND BEEN?

WHY, SHE'S MUCH PRETTIER THAN YOU!

WH-WHAT...??

LOOKS AT THOSE EYES! THOSE LIPS! THOSE...

WELL, JUST LOOK AT HER!

IS...THIS SOME KIND OF JOKE?

THAT... THAT'S A MANNEQUIN!

IT'S NOT ALIVE!!

NOT ALIVE...?

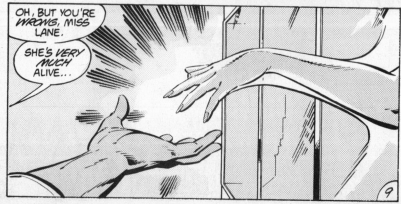

OH, BUT YOU'RE WRONG, MISS LANE.

SHE'S VERY MUCH ALIVE...

9

Alive... AND *EVERYTHING* ANY MAN COULD *WANT!*

OH, BEN *HONEY!* Y'ALL *DO* SAY TH' *SWEETEST* THAINGS!

AND NOW, IF YOU'LL *EXCUSE* US, MISS LANE, WE...

BEN, *HONEY!* *WAIT!* Y'ALL *CAIN'T* JEST *STROLL* OFF WITH ME!

THAT'D BE *STEALIN'!* BUT... BUT...

YOU'RE *RIGHT,* OF COURSE. PERHAPS...

PERHAPS AN *EXCHANGE* WOULD BE MORE *ACCEPTABLE!*

NO SIGN OF LOIS *ANYWHERE!*

AND THAT *BEN DEROY* CHARACTER SEEMS TO HAVE FADED INTO THE *OZONE,* TOO!

EEEEEEEEK

A WOMAN'S *SCREAM...*

COMING FROM *STACY'S* DEPARTMENT STORE.

YES THIS IS STACY'S

MISS...? WHAT IS IT? WHAT'S *WRONG?*

TH'... TH'... TH' *WINDOW DISPLAY!!*

I WAS S'POSED TO *CHANGE* THE SETUP T'DAY... BUT... BUT...

10

83

OH MY GOD!!

LOIS!! SHE'S BEEN TRANSFORMED INTO A MANNEQUIN!!

BUT... SHE'S WARM... STILL ALIVE!

WHAT IN BLAZES IS GOING ON AROUND HERE?

FIRST THAT GORILLA...

NOW LOIS...

YAHHHH!

HERE WE GO AGAIN!

MISS...CALL THE POLICE! GET MAGGIE SAWYER'S SPECIAL CRIMES UNIT DOWN HERE!

Y-YESSIR!

FLOOR RECTORY

MAGGIE'S TEAM CAN PROTECT LOIS UNTIL I CAN FIND SOME WAY TO RESTORE HER TO HUMAN FORM...

IF I CAN FIND A WAY!

NOW...WHERE DID THAT OTHER SCREAM COME FROM? A MAN'S SCREAM THIS TIME...

11

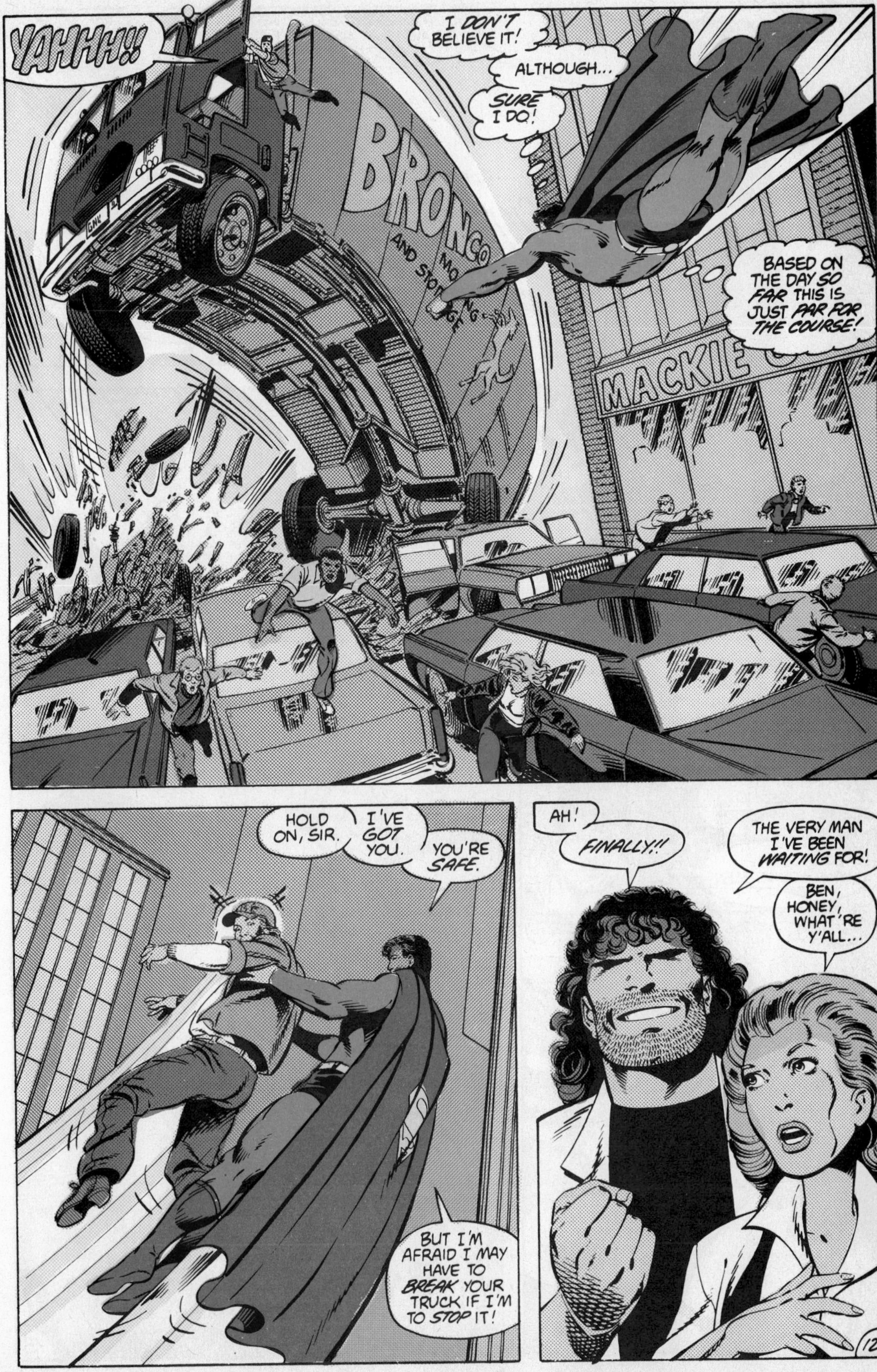

YAHHH!!
I DON'T BELIEVE IT!
ALTHOUGH...
SURE I DO!
BASED ON THE DAY SO FAR THIS IS JUST PAR FOR THE COURSE!
BRONCO
MACKIE
HOLD ON, SIR.
I'VE GOT YOU.
YOU'RE SAFE.
BUT I'M AFRAID I MAY HAVE TO BREAK YOUR TRUCK IF I'M TO STOP IT!
AH!
FINALLY!!
THE VERY MAN I'VE BEEN WAITING FOR!
BEN, HONEY, WHAT'RE Y'ALL...
12

SILENCE!

YOUR *USEFULNESS* TO ME IS AT AN *END!*

RETURN TO THE *FORM* IN WHICH I *FOUND* YOU!

BE :*:

AND NOW... GREETINGS, SUPERMAN! AT LAST WE *MEET,* FACE TO FACE!

DEROY! SO HE *IS* BEHIND ALL THIS!

BETTER NOT LET ON THAT WE'VE ALREADY *MET!* WHATEVER HIS *POWERS,* HE DOESN'T SEEM TO REALIZE I'M *CLARK KENT.*

YOU'RE A LITTLE TC:? PLEASED TO SEE ME, STRANGER...

CONSIDERING WHAT YOU'VE BEEN *UP* TO.

NOT AT ALL, SUPERMAN. ALL THIS WAS FOR *YOUR* BENEFIT.

TO *LURE* YOU INTO THE *OPEN...*

AND NOW YOU'RE HERE...

I HAVE NO FURTHER NEED OF THIS CUMBER-SOME *DISGUISE!*

WHAT IN...???

WHO *ARE* YOU!?!?

POINK!

13

MY *REAL* NAME WOULD NEVER *TRANSLATE* INTO YOUR CLUMSY EARTH LANGUAGES.

ALL YOU NEED TO KNOW IS THAT I'M FROM A *PARALLEL DIMENSION*.

YOU'D CALL IT... THE *FIFTH DIMENSION!*

AND I'VE BEEN *OBSERVING* YOUR PUNY LITTLE *THIRD DIMENSION* FOR QUITE SOME TIME NOW.

LONG ENOUGH TO KNOW MY SUPERIOR *5-D BRAIN* WILL MAKE ME THE MOST *POWERFUL* BEING ON THIS PLANET.

ALL *YOU* HAVE TO DO, SUPERMAN, IS *STOP ME!*

STOP...? YOU...?

YES. YOU SEE, I'M A *GAMESTER*, SUPERMAN. A *GAMBLER*.

AND I THINK *YOU* CAN PROVIDE ME WITH SOME OF THE *CHALLENGE* MY OWN WORLD HAS *LOST!*

WITH MY *POWERS* I CAN *ALTER YOU* AT WILL!

I CAN MAKE YOU *OLD*...

OF COURSE... IT WON'T BE *EASY* FOR YOU.

OR *FAT*...

OR *STUPID*...

...*DAHR*...

OR JUST... *STRANGE*...

14

BUT THAT'S TOO *EASY!*

TELL YOU WHAT I'LL *DO*, SUPERMAN. I'LL MAKE THIS *FAIR.*

I'LL CHALLENGE YOU TO *THE NAME GAME.*

ALL YOU HAVE TO DO IS GET ME TO *WRITE, SPELL,* OR *SAY* MY NAME *BACKWARDS!*

THAT'S *ALL,* HM? UNFORTUNATELY, ACCORDING TO YOU, YOUR NAME WON'T *TRANSLATE* INTO ANY HUMAN TONGUE!

TRUE ENOUGH. TRUE ENOUGH.

BUT I *DO* WANT YOU TO HAVE A *SPORTING CHANCE,* SUPERMAN.

SO...LET'S *MAKE UP* A NAME!

RIGHT HERE AND NOW!

HE...HE TRANSFORMED THAT *BILLBOARD* ILLUSTRATION INTO A *REAL* TYPEWRITER!

THERE MUST BE *NO LIMIT* TO HIS POWERS!!

THERE YOU ARE, SUPERMAN! *MIX-YEZ-PITTLE-ICK!!*

FROM NOW ON I'M *MISTER MXYZPTLK!!*

mxyzptlk

GET ME TO USE IT *BACKWARDS,* AND I'LL RETURN TO MY HOME DIMENSION...

AND ALL THE EFFECTS OF MY *VISIT* WILL VANISH WITH ME!

15

AND *SO FAR* THOSE EFFECTS HAVE BEEN *PIDDLING!*

TIME TO GET *SERIOUS,* I THINK!

SNIK! SNAK!

OH MY GOD!

HE'S *ANIMATED* THE *DAILY PLANET* BUILDING!!

MXYZPTLK...

STOP!! THERE ARE HUNDREDS OF *PEOPLE* IN THAT BUILDING!

WITH MY *X-RAY VISION* I CAN SEE THEM BEING TOSSED ABOUT LIKE CONFETTI IN A BOX!

OH, *FIDDLE FADDLE!* YOU 3-D LIFEFORMS ARE A *DIME* A DOZEN!

♪ *KLTPZ* ♪

HE'S... *TEASING* ME! SINGING *PART* OF HIS "*NAME*" BACKWARDS!

BUT...

WHAT IN *BLAZES* CAN I *DO!?!* HOW DO I *STOP* THE *PLANET* BUILDING...

WITHOUT *KILLING* PEOPLE INSIDE IT??

16

OH, *GREAT!* MXYZPTLK IMBUED THE BUILDING WITH A *CHILD'S* MENTALITY!

IT'S MAKING A GRAB FOR THE *WLEX* BLIMP!

IT THINKS IT'S SOME KIND OF *TOY!*

GOT TO *PUSH* IT OUT OF HIS REACH!

OH NO!

THE BUILDING'S THROWING A *TANTRUM!*

AND ITS *TEARS* ARE CAUSING A *FLASH FLOOD!*

HA HA HA HA

17

90

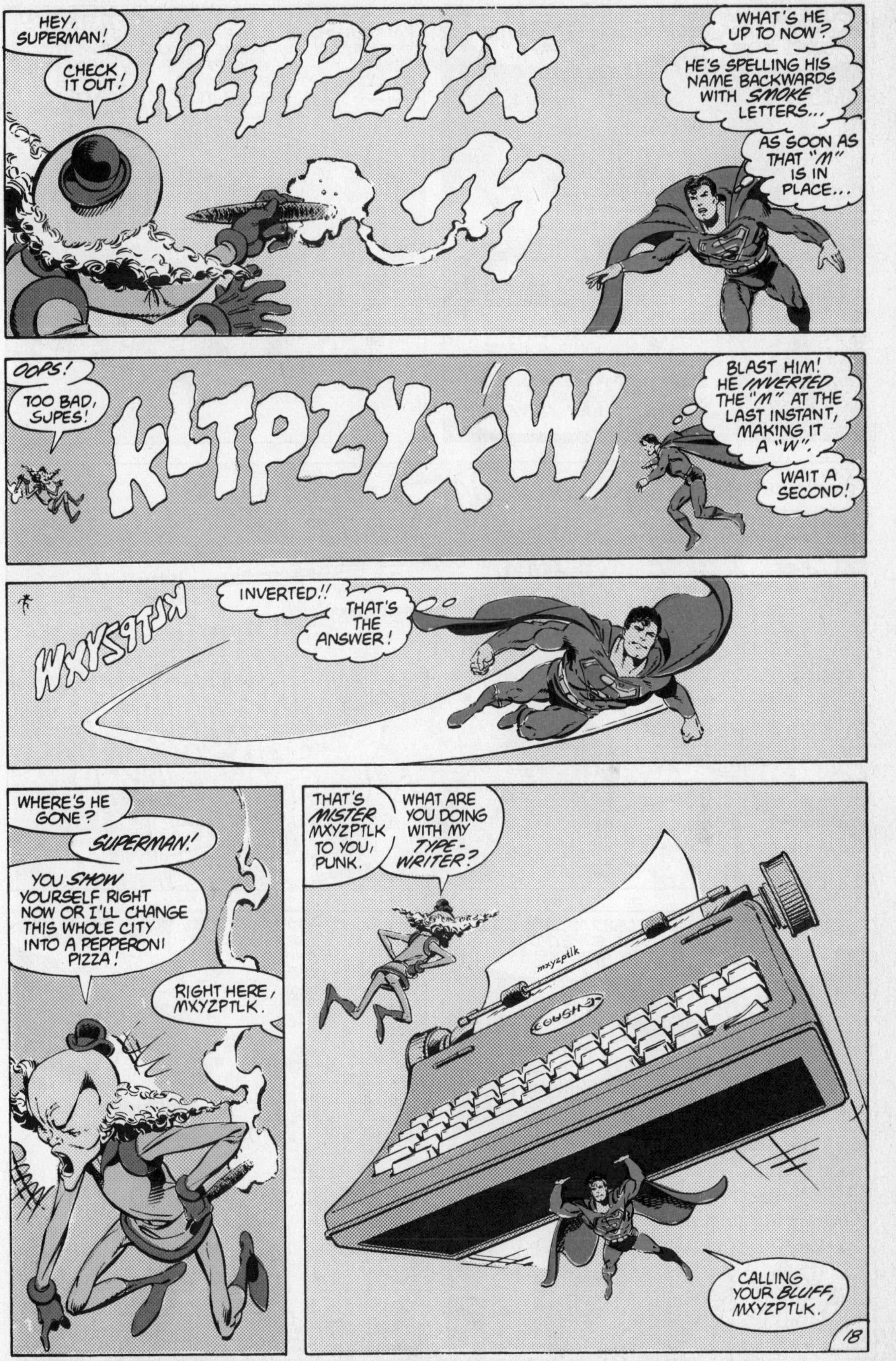

HEY, SUPERMAN!
CHECK IT OUT!
KLTPZYX
M
WHAT'S HE UP TO NOW?
HE'S SPELLING HIS NAME BACKWARDS WITH SMOKE LETTERS...
AS SOON AS THAT "M" IS IN PLACE...
OOPS!
TOO BAD, SUPES!
KLTPZYXW
BLAST HIM! HE INVERTED THE "M" AT THE LAST INSTANT, MAKING IT A "W".
WAIT A SECOND!
INVERTED!! THAT'S THE ANSWER!
WHERE'S HE GONE?
SUPERMAN!
YOU SHOW YOURSELF RIGHT NOW OR I'LL CHANGE THIS WHOLE CITY INTO A PEPPERONI PIZZA!
RIGHT HERE, MXYZPTLK.
THAT'S MISTER MXYZPTLK TO YOU, PUNK.
WHAT ARE YOU DOING WITH MY TYPE-WRITER?
mxyzptlk
CALLING YOUR BLUFF, MXYZPTLK.
18

YOU'VE BEEN MAKING ALL THIS *NOISE* ABOUT BEING *FAIR*.

CHALLENGING ME TO YOUR SO-CALLED *"NAME GAME".*

BUT *"MXYZPTLK"* ISN'T A NAME! A NAME IS SOMETHING THAT *REPRESENTS* A PERSON, IT'S NOT JUST *LETTERS*.

ALL YOU DID WAS HIT A BUNCH OF TYPEWRITER KEYS AT RANDOM.

FOR *"MXYZPTLK"* TO BE A REAL *NAME* IT WOULD HAVE TO HAVE BEEN CREATED *DELIBERATELY.*

I'M BETTING YOU CAN'T REPEAT YOUR RANDOM STRIKING TO PRODUCE THE *SAME SEQUENCE OF LETTERS!*

OH, WHAT *POPPYCOCK!*

LOOK!

IT'S *EAS...*

KLIK KLAK

kltpzyxm

KLIK KLAKETTY KLAK

EEP!

KLTPZYXM!!

IT CAN'T BE!

I USED MY MAGIC TO MAKE SURE I'D HIT THE RIGHT KEYS!!

BUT YOU *DIDN'T.*

SO LONG, *MXYZPTLK!*

ALL RIGHT, SUPERMAN.

YOU *WIN* THIS ONE!

AND I'LL KEEP MY *WORD* AND *LEAVE!*

BUT I'LL BE *BACK!*

COUNT ON IT, SUPERMAN!

"COUNT ON IT!!"

SO...HE'S GONE, SUPERMAN...

BUT NOT FOR GOOD?

NO...BUT FOR AT LEAST *90 DAYS*, I'D SAY.

I TALKED TO SOME OF THE *THEORETICAL PHYSICS* BOYS OVER AT THE *UNIVERSITY OF METROPOLIS.*

THEY SAY THAT'S THE NEXT TIME THERE WILL BE AN *OPTIMUM TRANSFER INTERFACE* BETWEEN US AND THE FIFTH DIMENSION.

BUT... HOW ARE *YOU,* LOIS?

STILL... *OFF.* CAN'T QUITE PUT IT INTO WORDS. COMING TO MY SENSES IN A DEPARTMENT STORE WINDOW DRESSED IN A BIKINI...

WELL...GIVEN THAT THE LAST THING I REMEMBERED *BEFORE* THAT WAS TURNING TO SPEAK TO CLARK KENT IN THE CITY ROOM...

IT WAS A BIT.... UN-NERVING, SUPERMAN.

UNNERVING...

YES. I GUESS THAT WOULD BE A WORD FOR IT. THE *PHYSICAL* EFFECTS OF MISTER MXYZPTLK'S VISIT ARE ALL GONE...

YOU'RE HUMAN AGAIN, THE PLANET BUILDING IS BACK IN PLACE...

THAT BUCKING BRONCO TRUCK IS JUST A TRUCK AGAIN.

BUT THE *PSYCHIATRIC WING* OF THIS HOSPITAL MAY HAVE TO OPEN A NEW WARD TO DEAL WITH ALL THE *TRAUMA* MXYZPTLK UNLEASHED.

THE THINGS HE DID LEFT *DEEPER SCARS* THAN JUST PHYSICAL INJURY.

I'LL TELL THE WORLD!

BUT... I'M STILL NOT SURE I UNDERSTAND JUST HOW YOU GOT RID OF HIM.

THAT WAS THE *EASY* PART, ONCE I FIGURED IT OUT. THE GIANT TYPEWRITER WORKED JUST LIKE A *REAL* ONE.

I SIMPLY *RE-WIRED* THE INSIDES AT SUPER-SPEED. WHEN HE HIT THE "M" KEY IT MADE A "K", THE "X" MADE AN "L", AND SO ON.

YOU SEE, I WAS *DEPENDING* ON HIM TO *CHEAT,* TO USE HIS *POWERS* TO STRIKE THE CORRECT KEYS *"AT RANDOM".*

AND WHEN HE DID...

M-X-Y-Z-P-T-L-K CAME OUT K-L-T-P-Z-Y-X-M!

AND HE *LOST!* 20

$4.25, LADY.

HERE'S A *FIVER.* KEEP THE *CHANGE.*

I SURE HOPE THIS ISN'T A *WASTE OF TIME.*

I'M JUST *ASSUMING* HE'S EVEN *HOME.*

344 CLINTON

MISS LANE!

NICE T'BE *SEEIN'* YOU AGAIN.

SHALL I BE *RINGIN'* MR. KENT?

ER...NO THANKS, MR. HARRIGAN. LET ME *SURPRISE* HIM.

GOOD, HE'S HOME!

NOW ALL I NEED TO WORRY ABOUT IS *WHY* I'M DOING THIS.

I *COULD* TELL MYSELF IT'S BECAUSE THAT *MIXELY-PLIT* CHARACTER CHEATED KENT OUT OF A *LUNCH...*

BUT THAT'S NOT *QUITE* AN EXPLANATION OF WHY I'D GET IT INTO MY HEAD TO COME OVER HERE AND COOK HIM *DINNER.*

COULD IT BE AFTER ALL THESE YEARS HE'S FINALLY *GETTING TO ME* WITH HIS *WORLD'S SEXIEST BOY SCOUT* ROUTINE?

BZZZT

PECAN RICE

YES...

...LOIS...?!?

CAT...!?!

WHAT...??

WHY...??

PECAN RICE

21

CLARKIE'S IN THE *SHOWER*.

I WAS JUST GOING TO FIX HIM A NICE *DINNER*.

LOIS! THAT'S NOT WHAT *YOU'RE* HERE FOR, IS IT?

WHAT...??

OH...

NO!

I WAS... JUST... *PASSING*...

OH, *GOOD!* THEN YOU CAN *KEEP* PASSING, YES?

I.... I...

WHO WAS THAT AT THE *DOOR*, CAT?

OH, NOBODY *IMPORTANT*.

SOMEBODY WHO GOT OFF ON THE WRONG *FLOOR* WITHOUT *REALIZING*.

NOW, C'MON, CLARKIE. DINNER'S *HOT*...

AND *SO* AM *I*!

...*CAT*...

95

BYRNE / PLOT • SCHAFFENBERGER / PENCILS • STERN / SCRIPT • ORDWAY / INKS • OAKLEY / LETTERS • SCOTESE / COLORS

MY NAME IS **LOIS LANE.** I'M A REPORTER.

YOU'VE PROBABLY SEEN MY BY-LINE IN THE **DAILY PLANET**... JUST UNDER THE HEADLINES...

YOU DON'T GET THE BIG STORIES WITHOUT TAKING A FEW **RISKS.** BUT RIGHT NOW, IT LOOKED LIKE I'D TAKEN ONE TOO MANY!

THIS IS THE DAME I TOL' YA ABOUT, CHOLLY... SAID SHE WAS LOOKIN' FOR THE BOSS.

IZZAT SO?

EVERYTHING WOULDA BEEN FINE IF I HADN'T LOST MY WIG.

LOTSA FOLKS WANNA SEE MR. KOZAK. YOU DON'T LOOK MUCH LIKE HIS TYPE TO ME... MAYBE YOU'RE **MY** TYPE, HUH?

MAYBE...

...BUT I **DOUBT** IT!

ONE THING I'VE NOTICED OVER THE YEARS... MOST MEN WHO USE GUNS ARE LOST WITHOUT THEM. THERE ARE EXCEPTIONS, OF COURSE...

...LIKE THE **GREEN BERET** WHO TRAINED ME IN HAND-TO-HAND.

BUT THESE TWO WERE **FAR** FROM BEING IN HIS LEAGUE!

VERY **GOOD**, MS. LANE. VERY GOOD **INDEED!** I AM IMPRESSED... AND BELIEVE ME, I **DON'T** IMPRESS EASILY!

1

96

YES, DESPITE YOUR... DISTRACTING ATTIRE--

--I RECOGNIZED YOU IMMEDIATELY. YOU SEE, I SAW YOU ON *A.M. METROPOLIS* LAST MONTH... AND I NEVER FORGET A FACE.

GENTLEMAN GEORGE KOZAK WAS AS SLIPPERY AS THEY COME... A WHITE COLLAR CRIMINAL WHO'D GONE INTO EXTORTION BEFORE HE WAS CAUGHT.

SIX WEEKS AGO, HE'D ESCAPED POLICE CUSTODY IN ANOTHER CITY.

TWO NIGHTS AGO, I'D GOTTEN A TIP HE WAS IN TOWN... AND I SET OUT TO FIND HIM.

IT'S UNFORTUNATE THAT WE HAD TO MEET THIS WAY, MS. LANE. I MUST ASK YOU TO KEEP YOUR HANDS WHERE I CAN SEE THEM.

I ONCE INTERVIEWED A LAS VEGAS CHORUS GIRL WHO'D DEVELOPED HER OWN STYLE OF SELF-DEFENSE.

SHE COULD'VE TAUGHT THE GREEN BERETS A FEW THINGS!

I TIED THEM UP AS BEST I COULD, BUT KNOTS WERE NEVER MY STRONG SUIT. FORTUNATELY, THERE WAS A PAY PHONE DOWN THE BLOCK.

IF IT WAS WORK- ING, I HAD NOTHING TO WORRY ABOUT. THAT WAS A BIG "IF" FOR THIS NEIGHBORHOOD--

--BUT MY LUCK HELD. WITHIN MINUTES, KOZAK AND HIS GOONS WERE IN CUSTODY. I GAVE MY STATEMENT TO METROPOLIS'S FINEST, AND PHONED MY STORY TO THE COPY DESK.

THEN, A *REAL* MIRACLE HAPPENED... I ACTUALLY GOT A CAB TO STOP FOR ME IN *SUICIDE SLUM!*

TAKE ME TO THE *DAILY PLANET!*

2

ANY OTHER TIME, I WOULD HAVE CALLED IT A DAY. BUT THERE WAS A NEW KID MANNING THE COPY DESK, AND THINGS SOUNDED CONFUSED OVER THE LINE. THIS STORY WAS TOO IMPORTANT TO GET GARBLED...

...I FIGURED I'D BETTER STOP AT THE OFFICE, JUST TO PLAY IT SAFE.

THAT'S SOME OUTFIT, MISS LANE-- YOU GOIN' TO A *MASQUERADE?*

NOT EXACTLY, EDDIE... YOU CAN READ ALL ABOUT IT IN THE EVENING EDITION.

AFTERNOON, ALL-- WHAT'S ... NEWS?

DO YOU BELIEVE IT?

MAKES SENSE TO ME.

REAGAN MAKES SENSE TO YOU!

THE LUCKY STIFF!

LOIS! I DIDN'T EXPECT YOU IN!

I DIDN'T EXPECT ME IN EITHER, PERRY. WHAT'S ALL THE HUBBUB?

IT'S THIS STORY OUT OF BOSTON! MUST BE THE BIGGEST *LOVE STORY* SINCE EDWARD VIII GAVE UP THE THRONE OF ENGLAND TO MARRY WALLIS SIMPSON!

WE'RE TRYING TO GET MORE ON IT, BUT EVERY LINE BETWEEN HERE AND BOSTON HAS BEEN *JAMMED!*

S-SUPERMAN... AND *WONDER WOMAN?* I NEVER SUSPECTED--!

BOSTON GLOBE-LEADER

TRUE LOVE?

SUPER-ROMANCE OF THE CENTURY

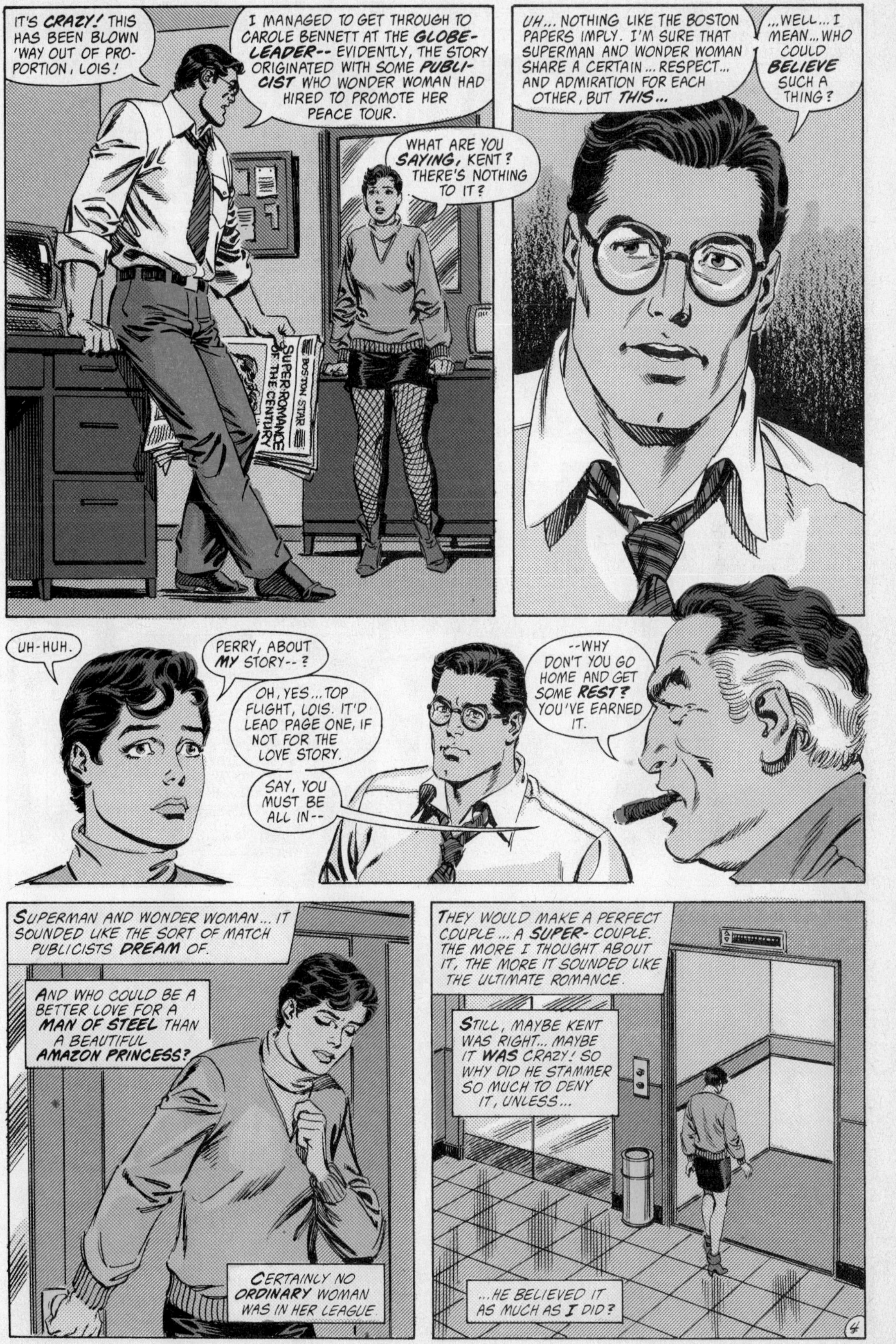

IT'S CRAZY! THIS HAS BEEN BLOWN 'WAY OUT OF PROPORTION, LOIS!
I MANAGED TO GET THROUGH TO CAROLE BENNETT AT THE GLOBE-LEADER-- EVIDENTLY, THE STORY ORIGINATED WITH SOME PUBLICIST WHO WONDER WOMAN HAD HIRED TO PROMOTE HER PEACE TOUR.
WHAT ARE YOU SAYING, KENT? THERE'S NOTHING TO IT?
BOSTON STAR
SUPER-ROMANCE OF THE CENTURY
UH... NOTHING LIKE THE BOSTON PAPERS IMPLY. I'M SURE THAT SUPERMAN AND WONDER WOMAN SHARE A CERTAIN... RESPECT... AND ADMIRATION FOR EACH OTHER, BUT THIS...
...WELL... I MEAN... WHO COULD BELIEVE SUCH A THING?
UH-HUH.
PERRY, ABOUT MY STORY--?
OH, YES... TOP FLIGHT, LOIS. IT'D LEAD PAGE ONE, IF NOT FOR THE LOVE STORY.
SAY, YOU MUST BE ALL IN--
--WHY DON'T YOU GO HOME AND GET SOME REST? YOU'VE EARNED IT.
SUPERMAN AND WONDER WOMAN... IT SOUNDED LIKE THE SORT OF MATCH PUBLICISTS DREAM OF.
AND WHO COULD BE A BETTER LOVE FOR A MAN OF STEEL THAN A BEAUTIFUL AMAZON PRINCESS?
CERTAINLY NO ORDINARY WOMAN WAS IN HER LEAGUE.
THEY WOULD MAKE A PERFECT COUPLE... A SUPER-COUPLE. THE MORE I THOUGHT ABOUT IT, THE MORE IT SOUNDED LIKE THE ULTIMATE ROMANCE.
STILL, MAYBE KENT WAS RIGHT... MAYBE IT WAS CRAZY! SO WHY DID HE STAMMER SO MUCH TO DENY IT, UNLESS...
...HE BELIEVED IT AS MUCH AS I DID?
4

IT'S FUNNY HOW EVENTS COME OUT OF NOWHERE AND TURN YOUR BRAIN INSIDE OUT.

I THOUGHT THAT NOTHING COULD SURPRISE ME MUCH ANYMORE, BUT THE STORY FROM BOSTON HIT HARD.

PRODUCE · FRUIT · WHOLESALE · RETAIL

CARMINE'S PRO

HOW HARD?

WELL, MY APARTMENT IS A RESPECTABLE DISTANCE FROM THE PLANET BUILDING-- BUT IT'S NOT ALL THAT FAR, SO I DECIDED TO WALK.

I WAS STILL WALKING AN HOUR LATER.

AFTER I LEFT THE PLANET, I MUST HAVE TOTALLY FOGGED OUT AND WALKED RIGHT PAST MY BUILDING.

BEFORE I KNEW, I WAS IN THE PARK... WITH NO RECOLLECTION OF ANYTHING I MIGHT HAVE PASSED ALONG THE WAY.

THAT SHOOK ME ENOUGH TO TAKE A CAB HOME.

I TRIED TELLING MYSELF IT WAS FATIGUE-- I HAD SPENT MOST OF THE PREVIOUS 48 HOURS TRACKING DOWN KOZAK, AFTER ALL. I JUST NEEDED A LITTLE REST.

BUT I COULDN'T SLEEP. I KEPT THINKING ABOUT WONDER WOMAN... HOW MUCH REST DOES SHE NEED? WILL SHE HAVE TO WORRY ABOUT GRAY HAIRS OR SMILE LINES?

WOULD SHE EVER EVEN GROW OLD?!

A COLUMNIST FOR A RIVAL PAPER ONCE GOT HIS NOSE OUT OF JOINT OVER THE NUMBER OF EXCLUSIVE SUPERMAN STORIES I LANDED, AND REFERRED TO ME IN PRINT AS "SUPERMAN'S GIRLFRIEND".

I HAD GOTTEN A LOT OF MILEAGE MAKING FUN OF THAT ITEM... BUT I'D ALSO WISHED IT WERE TRUE.

I'D THOUGHT I WAS OVER THAT.

JUST A FEW WEEKS AGO, CLARK KENT'S PARENTS TOLD ME THAT THEY'D SECRETLY RAISED SUPERMAN FROM A BABY...THAT HE AND KENT WERE LIKE STEP-BROTHERS.

I WAS OUTRAGED... I ACCUSED SUPERMAN AND KENT OF PLAYING ME FOR A FOOL ALL THESE YEARS. I WAS SO MAD, I STARTED TO WRITE THE WHOLE THING UP... AN EXPOSÉ ON SUPERMAN!

THANK GOD, I DESTROYED IT WHEN I COOLED OFF. IT WOULD HAVE BEEN A DEATH WARRANT FOR KENT'S PARENTS.

I HADN'T REALLY FINISHED COMING TO TERMS WITH ALL THAT YET... IT WAS SO RECENT.

AND NOW... THIS.

I KNEW I OUGHT TO FACE FACTS ... WRITE SUPERMAN OUT OF MY LIFE FOR GOOD, AND START THE NEXT CHAPTER.

AS IF I COULD FORGET SOMEONE LIKE HIM!

IF THERE WERE SOMEONE ELSE-- ANYONE ELSE-- MAYBE ...

NOK NOK

?!?

⑥

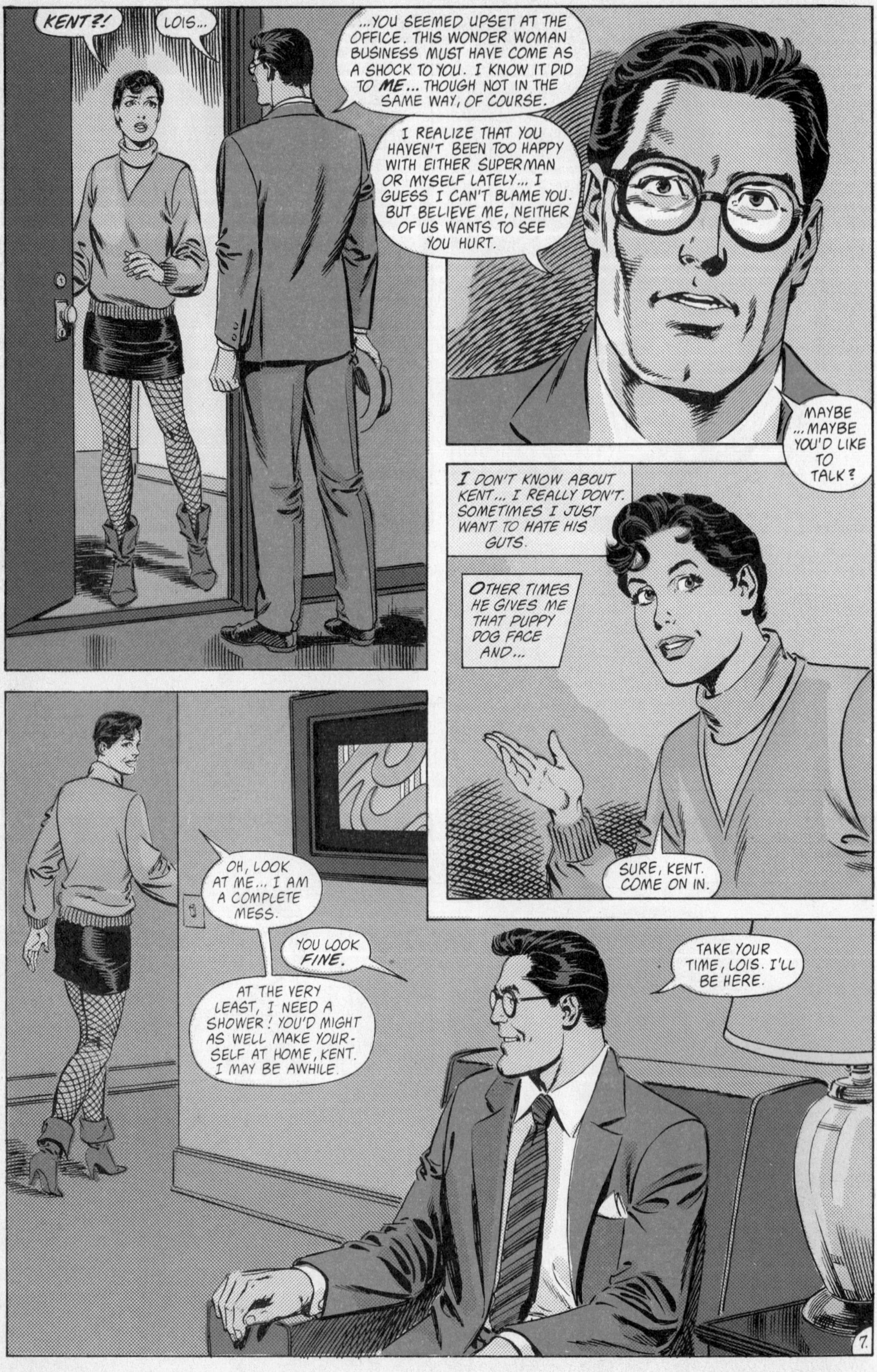
KENT?!
LOIS...
...YOU SEEMED UPSET AT THE OFFICE. THIS WONDER WOMAN BUSINESS MUST HAVE COME AS A SHOCK TO YOU. I KNOW IT DID TO ME... THOUGH NOT IN THE SAME WAY, OF COURSE.
I REALIZE THAT YOU HAVEN'T BEEN TOO HAPPY WITH EITHER SUPERMAN OR MYSELF LATELY... I GUESS I CAN'T BLAME YOU. BUT BELIEVE ME, NEITHER OF US WANTS TO SEE YOU HURT.
MAYBE ...MAYBE YOU'D LIKE TO TALK?
I DON'T KNOW ABOUT KENT... I REALLY DON'T. SOMETIMES I JUST WANT TO HATE HIS GUTS.
OTHER TIMES HE GIVES ME THAT PUPPY DOG FACE AND...
SURE, KENT. COME ON IN.
OH, LOOK AT ME... I AM A COMPLETE MESS.
YOU LOOK FINE.
AT THE VERY LEAST, I NEED A SHOWER! YOU'D MIGHT AS WELL MAKE YOUR-SELF AT HOME, KENT. I MAY BE AWHILE.
TAKE YOUR TIME, LOIS. I'LL BE HERE.
7.

ZEEEE-EEEEEEEEE

EH?

OH, NO-- THAT'S THE HYPERSONIC TONE FROM JIMMY OLSEN'S *SIGNAL WATCH!*

NOT NOW, JIM... OF ALL TIMES, *NOT NOW!*

I OUGHT TO... *NO.* JIMMY WOULDN'T SIGNAL ME WITHOUT GOOD REASON.

I CAN'T IGNORE A CALL FOR--

SUPERMAN!

MAYBE I'LL BE ABLE TO HANDLE THIS AND GET BACK BEFORE LOIS NOTICES THAT CLARK IS GONE.

SAY, CLARK, I HAD A THOUGHT...

...I DON'T KNOW ABOUT YOU, BUT I'M *FAMISHED.* WHILE I'M IN THE SHOWER, WHY DON'T YOU HOP DOWN TO EMILIO'S AND GET US A PIZZA... WITH THE WORKS?

KENT? HELLO?

KENT!

"I'LL BE HERE", HUH? OF ALL THE--!

YOU'RE ON MY LIST, MR. KENT! YOU... YOU... *OHH!!*

JERRY ORDWAY
WRITER / PENCILLER

DENNIS JANKE
INKER

ALBERT DeGUZMAN
LETTERER

THE ADVENTURES OF SUPERMAN
Created by
JERRY SIEGEL &
JOE SHUSTER

PETRA SCOTESE
COLORIST

RENÉE WITTERSTAETTER
ASSISTANT EDITOR

MIKE CARLIN
EDITOR

HEADHUNTER

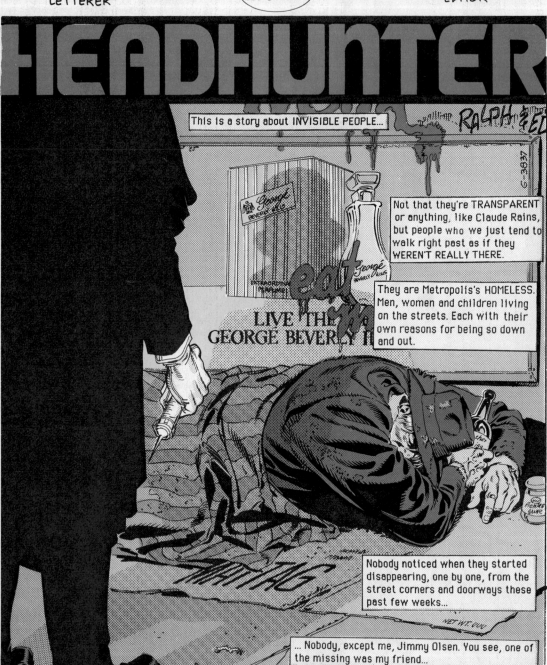

His name was PETE SHOEMAKER. You may have PASSED HIM at the subway entrance on 83rd street in BAKERLINE yourself. Until last TUESDAY that is.

HUH? WHO'S THAT?

Pete NEVER bothered anyone... and for the most part NO ONE bothered him. On cold nights, "Bakerline's Finest" would take him to a SHELTER. But Pete could take care of HIMSELF all alone just fine.

I AM YOUR SALVATION.

STAY AWAY!

He PREFERRED the street over the shelter, claiming the shelter was for BUMS. He never PANHANDLED from me-- Pete had an air of DIGNITY about him, despite his "situation."

I OFFER YOU A WAY OUT OF YOUR DESPAIR.

Seemingly comfortable with his lot in life, Pete would tell me, "an honest man's pillow was his peace of mind." Pete slept well, no doubt.

LET ME BE, MISTER... I DONE NOTHIN' TA YOU.

I want to know what happened to my FRIEND, Pete. I want to know what happened to the OTHERS!

DO NOT RUN FROM THIS.

NOOOOOO!

I'M HERE TO RELEASE YOU....

After much runaround I am pleased to say that Police officials have opened a missing persons file on Peter James Shoemaker at this reporter's behest...

...RELEASE YOU FROM THIS PITIFUL EXISTENCE!

WHAT DO YOU THINK OF IT SO FAR, MR. WHITE?

LOOK, OLSEN... I KNOW YOU'RE FRIENDS WITH THIS GUY, BUT THIS IS A PAGE TWENTY STORY AT BEST.

YOU'RE NOT A COLUMNIST... NOT YET, KID. YOU EVEN SPELLED "ALONE" WRONG.

MAYBE WE CAN GET LOIS TO--

CHIEF... NO! LET ME FIX IT. OKAY?

REALLY... CLARK'S BEEN GONE FOR DAYS, AND LOIS IS TOO BUSY AND...

OKAY... I'M SORRY I CALLED YOU CHIEF.

HMMMMPH! LOOK, JIMMY... THIS STORY NEEDS STRUCTURE-- ANY FORM OF STRUCTURE... IT HAS TO GO SOMEWHERE...

WHY DON'T YOU GO SEE INSPECTOR HENDERSON AND SEE IF THERE'S ANYTHING NEW TO REPORT... OKAY...

I KNOW I CAN DO THIS. I JUST NEED SOME PRACTICE. IT'S HARD TO WRITE "JUST THE FACTS" WHEN YOU'RE WRITING ABOUT SOMEONE YOU KNOW.

CAN'T SHAKE THE FEELING THAT ANY NEWS HENDERSON HAS ON PETE WILL BE BAD NEWS.

AND OLSEN... REMEMBER WHAT I TOLD YOU ABOUT WEARING A TIE TO THE OFFICE?

SORRY, MR. WHITE. I FORGOT TODAY.

I'VE GOT TO GET SOME NEW NECKTIES...

TOO MANY THINGS ON MY MIND LATELY...

BEING MISTAKEN FOR SOME KIND OF CARROT-TOPPED GOD BY TEHRA AND THE EXILES IN THE MID-EAST *...

AND MY MOM'S STILL OBSESSED WITH FINDING MY DAD! ** WHEN WILL THIS ALL--

*ADVENTURES OF SUPERMAN #443.

**ADVENTURES OF SUPERMAN #442.

--END?!

BUT I'VE ONLY GOT A FIFTY.

SORRY, LADY...

CAT? HAVING A PROBLEM?

OH... JIMMY, DAR-LING! DO YOU THINK YOU COULD... PAY THIS FARE FOR ME?

I JUST DON'T SEEM TO HAVE THE CORRECT CHANGE.

THANKS, SWEETIE! I'LL BUY YOU A DRINK OR SOMETHING AFTER WORK AT SAM'S BAR, SAY, SIX-ISH. 'KAY?

BUT CAT... I'M NOT OLD ENOUGH...

DARN.. HOW MUCH?

SIX-FIFTY, JUNIOR.

CAT!

GOOD *MORNING*, FELLOW SCRIBES! OR SHOULD I SAY GOOD *AFTERNOON*?

WHAT'S SO GOOD ABOUT IT?

LOOK, LOIS, YOU KNOW HE'S SLIME AND I KNOW HE'S SLIME-- BUT OUR EDITORIALS ARE IN THE BACK OF THE PAPER--NOT ON PAGE ONE!

BUT, PERRY...

HI, LOIS!

FINE! FINE! PUT IT ON THE BACK PAGE! HELP HIM COVER HIMSELF UP! FINE!

LOIS! GETTING ALL BENT OUT OF SHAPE'S NOT GOING TO MAKE ME CHANGE MY MIND.

BOY, SHE STILL *DOES* HATE ME... SHE ACTS LIKE I'M NOT EVEN HERE!

OH, NO...NOT YOU TOO...CAN I HAVE JUST ONE MINUTE, PERRY?

LIFE'S *TOUGH* THAT WAY, GRANT. NOW, IF YOU'LL--

YA GOT ME FOR FIVE, GRANT... IN MY OFFICE...

PERRY, I DON'T THINK THIS IS WORKING OUT... *NO ONE* LIKES ME HERE AT THE PLANET... I DON'T FIT *IN* HERE...

YOU'RE STILL NEW HERE. THESE PEOPLE HAVE BEEN THROUGH A LOT TOGETHER-- THEY'RE LIKE FAMILY.

BESIDES, THIS *IS* THE *CITY* ROOM...YOU WORK IN THE *FEATURES* DEPARTMENT!

THAT'S NOT MY POINT.

LOOK, MISS GRANT--

CAT! AND TELL ME WHAT YOU *REALLY* THINK, PERRY... I NEED TO KNOW.

OKAY, CAT...

FIRST OFF, I *DON'T* LIKE MY REPORTERS INVOLVED IN OFFICE ROMANCES. IT'S TOO *DISRUPTIVE*. WHEN THINGS GO *BAD*, WE ALL SUFFER!

JUST LOOK AT CLARK AND LOIS!

SINCE YOU'VE BEEN HERE *I'VE* SEEN YOU LITERALLY *THROW* YOURSELF AT CLARK--RIGHT IN FRONT OF LOIS...*SEVERAL TIMES!*

GREAT CAESAR'S GHOST, YOU'VE EVEN STARTED PLAYING YOUNG OLSEN FOR A FOOL!

BUT JIMMY'S A CUTE KID.

HE'S ONE OF MY REPORTERS!

WHAT YOU'RE DOING TO OLSEN IS DOWN RIGHT MEAN! AND I'M *NOT* ALONE IN THINKING THIS!

BUT I *DO* LIKE JIMMY...

UMMM, I THINK I'D LIKE TO GET BACK TO MY WORK, SIR... IF YOU'LL--

NO. YOU ASKED FOR MY OPINIONS AND, BY GUM, YOU'LL HEAR ME OUT!

IT'S NO SECRET, CAT, THAT YOU'VE ALSO BEEN COMING TO WORK HALF IN THE BAG LATELY-- *DRUNK*, TO PUT IT BLUNTLY!

WHO'S SAYING THAT? HAS SOMEONE BEEN TELLING YOU I HAVE A PROBLEM? BECAUSE I *DON'T.* I SWEAR!

YOU'RE WRONG MISS GRANT. YOU *DO* HAVE A PROBLEM... *ME!*

I WILL NOT STAND FOR *ANYONE* COMING TO MY CITY ROOM STINKING OF BOOZE!

I'VE SEEN TOO MANY *GOOD* REPORTERS *DROWN* THEIR CAREERS IN A *BOTTLE,* MISS GRANT.

FOR GOD'S SAKE, YOU OWE IT TO YOUR *SON* TO BE THERE FOR HIM WHILE HE'S *GROWING UP!*

COME ON, MISS GRANT... MY WIFE ALICE READS YOUR COLUMN... AND SHE TELLS ME IT'S *GOOD,* TOO...

AND IN ALL OUR YEARS TOGETHER I'VE LEARNED SHE'S USUALLY *RIGHT!*

PLEASE DON'T MAKE ALICE *WRONG,* MISS-- CAT-- PLEASE... FOR YOUR OWN SAKE.

PERRY WHITE EDITOR

THANK YOU, MR. WHITE. GOOD AFTERNOON, SIR.

MIDTOWN POLICE STATION...

CAT SURE *SUCKERED* ME INTO PAYING THAT CAB FARE!

BOY, FOR A WHILE THERE I ACTUALLY THOUGHT SHE WAS SOMETHING *HOT...*

BUT SHE'S CHANGED *THAT* PERCEPTION! SARAH OLSEN'S SON MAY BE A BIG DOPE, BUT HE AIN'T NO FOOL!

BILL, I'VE GOT A JIMMY OLSEN WAITING TO SEE YOU...

INSPECTOR WM. HENDERSON

I'M IN A HURRY... BUT... OH, OKAY, SEND HIM IN. MIGHT AS WELL GET THIS OVER WITH.

DET. SCHMIDT

IN
OUT

TAKE A BITE OUT OF CRIME WITH NEIGHBORHOOD WATCH PATROLS!

HI, INSPECTOR... LONG TIME NO SEE...

OLSEN...HOW'S THE PLANET'S ACE REPORTER DOIN'?

JUST THOUGHT I'D STOP BY AND SEE IF THERE WERE ANY NEW DEVELOPMENTS CONCERNING PETE.

'FRAID SO, KID.

WE FOUND A BODY MATCHING PETE'S DESCRIPTION IN A DOWNTOWN PARKING GARAGE.

WE'RE WAITING ON THE CORONER'S REPORT, BUT I'LL TELL YOU THIS...

PETE SHOEMAKER'S DEATH'S JUST THE TIP OF THE ICEBERG!

IN THE PAST TWENTY-FOUR HOURS THREE OTHER BODIES HAVE BEEN FOUND. TWO IN THE BOWERY AND ONE IN SUICIDE SLUM.

THERE'S EVEN A THIN THREAD THAT TIES THEM ALL TOGETHER.

THEY ALL HAD SOME HEAVY-DUTY NEEDLE MARKS AT THE BASE OF THEIR SPINES!

I'M BETTING THAT YOUR FRIEND'S AUTOPSY REPORT SHOWS THE SAME THING.

POOR PETE.

OUR INVESTIGATION TURNED UP SOME INTERESTING STUFF ON SHOEMAKER, THOUGH.

HE HAS FAMILY IN CLEVELAND-- EVEN PLAYED PRO BASEBALL FOR A WHILE....

HE SPENT MANY YEARS RIDING THE RAILS HOBO-STYLE, TOO.

HE PLAYED PRO BASEBALL?

THE HOBO PART'S WHAT INTRIGUED ME. YOU SEE, HOBOS HAVE THEIR OWN SIGN LANGUAGE--KIND OF A CODE...

THEY'D MARK A HOUSE WHERE ONE HOBO GOT A FREE HANDOUT, SO THAT OTHERS COMING BY AFTERWARD KNEW EXACTLY WHO IN THE AREA WAS AN EASY TOUCH.

TRANSIENTS COULD EASILY TELL BY THESE SIGNS WHETHER A TOWN WAS KIND TO STRANGERS.

PETE HAD APPARENTLY SCRAWLED THIS IN THE SIDEWALK WHEN HE WAS INITIALLY ABDUCTED AT 83RD STREET IN BAKERLINE.

AND I THINK THIS IS A DRAWING OF THE MAN WHO KILLED HIM.

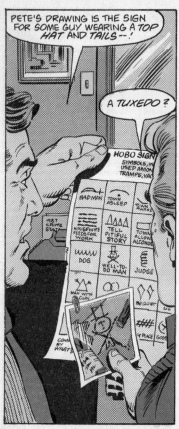

PETE'S DRAWING IS THE SIGN FOR SOME GUY WEARING A *TOP HAT* AND TAILS--!

A *TUXEDO?*

HOBO SIGN
Symbols used among tramps, vag...

BAD MAN | TOWN ASLEEP | TOWN MARS...
HOUSEWIFE FEEDS FOR WORK | TELL PITIFUL STORY | TOWN ALLOWS ALCOHOL
DOG | WELL-TO-DO MAN | JUDGE
MAN WITH GUN | | BEQUEST
| | SAFE PLACE GOOD

YUP, AND I HAVE A REAL HARD TIME BELIEVING SOME KILLER'S MAKING LIKE *FRED ASTAIRE*-- BUT AT LEAST IT'S A *LEAD!*

HAVE YOU RUN ANY OF THIS PAST *MAGGIE SAWYER* AT S.C.U.?*

*SPECIAL CRIMES UNIT.

SHE AND I DON'T *GET ALONG* VERY WELL. WHY? GOT ANY *INSPIRATIONS?*

NOT REALLY. JUST THOUGHT *SHE* MIGHT HAVE!

I'LL TALK TO HER...

...AND, *KID...*

"STAY OUT OF *TROUBLE,* OKAY?"

NO. *NO.!!* I'M *FAILING...*

THE HEADACHES...

...THEY'RE *BACK!...* WORSE THAN *BEFORE!!*

I WILL NOT-- *CANNOT* LET THIS STOP ME *NOW*-- NOT NOW THAT I'VE *FINALLY GAINED CONTROL* OVER THIS PITIFUL *BODY!!*

THIS WORLD HAS YET TO *REEL* BEFORE THE POWER OF

BRAINIAC

THE *HUMAN'S* FORM IS *REJECTING* MY ALIEN *LIFEFORCE*-- I CANNOT *ALLOW* IT TO CONTINUE ANY FURTHER ...

... BUT MY EARLY MINISTERINGS HAVE HAD NO EFFECT!

MILTON FINE, A *DRUNKEN FOOL*, USED HIS OWN *WONDROUS* MIND TO REACH OUT THROUGH THE *COSMOS*--

--ULTIMATELY LOCATING ME, *VRIL DOX*--A *DEMOLISHED* BEING'S DISEMBODIED INTELLECT FROM THE PLANET *COLU!* *

* IN ADVENTURES OF SUPERMAN #438.

FINE'S WILL WAS *WEAK*, ALLOWING ME TO EASILY *COMMANDEER* HIS BODY. --BUT NOW HIS BODY WEAKENS AS WELL AS MY POWERFUL ESSENCE *RAVAGES* IT!

SPINAL FLUID DIDN'T HOLD THE KEY TO SALVAGING THIS *HOST-BODY.* I'LL HAVE TO TRY SOMETHING MORE *DRASTIC!* I MUST SEARCH FOR MORE *TEST SUBJECTS*--AT *THIS* TIME...

CRASH!

I WILL HAVE THEIR ENTIRE *BRAINS!*

HA HA HA HA HA

I THOUGHT YOU HAD MORE BRAINS THAN *THAT*, JOSE!

LOIS LANE'S *NOT* THE TYPE TO *PITY* YOU! SHE CARES FOR YOU AN AWFUL *LOT*.

YOU THINK THAT SHE'S DOING ALL THIS BECAUSE YOU *SAVED HER LIFE*? SUPERMAN DOES THAT EVERY DAY, AND SHE'S *NOT DATING HIM*!

SUPERMAN DOESN'T GET *PARALYZED* FROM THE *WAIST DOWN* BATTLING STOOGES LIKE *COMBATTOR*-- I DID!

SHE FEELS SHE *OWES* ME, JERRY, AND I CAN'T HAVE HER THAT WAY!

YOU'RE *DEAD WRONG*, JOSE.

LOIS IS *BETTER* THAN THAT!

WHICH IS *WHY* SHE DESERVES *BETTER* THAN THAT!

SOMETHING LIKE A *WHOLE MAN*!

DON'T YOU THINK SHE'S CAPABLE OF MAKING THAT CHOICE ON HER *OWN*?

BESIDES, WE'RE JUST TALKING ABOUT A *DATE*!

I'M *NOT GOING OUT*!

I'M SICK OF BEING *CARRIED UP* AND DOWN THESE STAIRS LIKE A *BABY*-- ESPECIALLY BY LOIS!!

I'LL GO OUT *IF* AND *WHEN* I CAN NAVIGATE THE STAIRS BY *MYSELF*!

THAT SOCIAL SERVICES AGENCY *HAD* A PLACE FOR YOU *WITH* WHEELCHAIR RAMPS, BUT YOU *TURNED* THEM *DOWN*!

THIS IS MY HOME!

RRIIIINNNG!!

JOSE, THIS SOUNDS IMPORTANT! SOMEONE FROM *ADVANCED RESEARCH LABORATORIES*.

I'M *SICK* OF THESE CALLS! GIVE IT TO ME, I'LL HANDLE IT!

THIS IS MR. DELGADO-- LOOK, IF YOU'RE *ANOTHER* CALLER SELLING *MOTORIZED* WHEELCHAIRS--

I ASSURE YOU I AM *NOT* SELLING WHEELCHAIRS, MR. DELGADO. JUST THE *OPPOSITE*, IN FACT. I'M OFFERING YOU THE CHANCE TO GET OUT OF YOUR WHEELCHAIR FOR GOOD. LEAVE IT COMPLETELY BEHIND.

IS THIS YOUR IDEA OF A *JOKE*? WHO IS THIS?

I AM ADELE DE HAVENET, MR. DELGADO, AND *A.R.L.* IS LEGITIMATE, AS IS OUR OFFER TO YOU...

GO ON...

RUN, EUGENE! IT'S THAT REPORTER WHO PUT JIM IN TRACTION!

HOPE YOU DEADBEATS AREN'T STILL HARASSING OLD WOMEN?

WE DIDN'T DO NUTHIN' TO HER-- WE SWEAR!

ELSA'S BEEN GONE FOR DAYS! *NOBODY'S* SEEN HER!

NO!

WE HAVE DONE SOME *PROMISING* WORK ON SPINAL INJURIES USING COMPUTER MICROCHIPS, MR. DELGADO. FRANKLY, WE FEEL EXTREMELY CONFIDENT WE CAN HELP YOU.

HMMM. WONDER IF I SHOULD *BOTHER* JOSE WITH ELSA'S DISAPPEARANCE?

WE BELIEVE WE CAN GET YOU *UP* AND *WALKING* AGAIN, MR. DELGADO.

MR. DELGADO? HELLO?

LOIS, HI!

OH, HELLO.

IF THIS IS ON THE *LEVEL*, MS. DE HAVENET, YOU'VE HOOKED YOURSELF A CUSTOMER!

"IT'S SO QUIET UP THERE. I'M WORRIED ABOUT CLARK."

"HE'S BEEN SITTING IN THE DARK LIKE THAT ALL MORNING."

"HE'S IN A BAD WAY. IT'S KILLING ME TO SEE HIM LIKE THIS."

"HE'S ALWAYS COME TO US BEFORE WITH HIS PROBLEMS. MUST BE WRESTLING WITH SOMETHING BIG THIS TIME, MA."

"WHY DON'T YOU SEE IF HE NEEDS ANYTHING?"

KNOCK KNOCK

CLARK? YOUR MA AND I WERE-- WELL, WE'RE WORRIED.

SON?

I JUST THOUGHT-- WELL, WHEN YOU'RE READY... I WANT YOU TO KNOW THAT WE'RE HERE FOR YOU.

I KNOW-- I JUST CAN'T TALK--YET.

I NEED TO... TO JUST SIT HERE-- IN MY ROOM--WITH ALL MY THINGS ...MEMENTOES OF SMALLVILLE SURROUNDING ME--REASSURING ME.

I HAVE TO PRETEND I DON'T HEAR THE REST OF THE WORLD OUT THERE... PRETEND THAT NO ONE NEEDS ME JUST NOW...

I HAVE TO BE ALONE-- TO SEE IF I CAN STILL LIVE WITH MYSELF... WITH WHAT I'VE DONE.

ESCAPED? HOW COULD YOU LET A DANGEROUS GUY LIKE THAT *GET AWAY*?

CAPTAIN MARGARET SAWYER SPECIAL CRIMES UNIT

BACK OFF, OLSEN! I TOLD YOU I'D GIVE YOU SOME INFO ON THIS, SO JUST SETTLE DOWN...

BASICALLY, I AGREE WITH YOU--HE *SHOULD* STILL BE IN OUR CUSTODY...

BUT IT'S LIKE THIS, JUNIOR--FOR EVERY *SUPERMAN*, WE'VE GOT AT LEAST A *DOZEN* SUPER-VILLAIN TYPES TO CONTEND WITH. *STRYKER'S ISLAND* IS LOADED WITH GUYS LIKE THE JOKER... THE PRANKSTER... THE--

WHAT'VE THEY GOT TO DO WITH *MILTON FINE*?

MILTON FINE, A.K.A. "THE AMAZING BRAINIAC," WAS SHIPPED OFF TO THE PSYCHO WARD AT BELLEVUE FOR OBSERVATION.

HIS OUTBURST AT THE CIRCUS WAS CONSIDERED AN *ISOLATED* INCIDENT.

THANKS TO SUPERMAN, WHO STOPPED HIM! FORGET THAT WITHOUT JANET JONES, FINE'S ASSISTANT, WHO SEEMED TO HAVE SOME KIND OF WEIRD *INFLUENCE* OVER HIM--EVEN SUPERMAN MIGHT NOT HAVE BEEN ABLE TO STOP HIM!

SO WHEN I HEARD OF *HER* DEATH, * I WONDERED HOW THAT MIGHT AFFECT BRAINIAC'S MIND.

* SUPERMAN #20.

EXCUSE ME, CAPTAIN SAWYER. THIS IS DOCTOR HOWARD, FINE'S DOCTOR AT BELLEVUE.

JUST THE MAN I WANT TO SEE... ABOUT YOUR DIAGNOSIS-- CAN YOU ELABORATE FOR ME?

CAPTAIN MARGARET SAWYER SPECIAL CRIMES UNIT

YOU MEAN THE SCHIZOPHRENIC CATEGORIZATION? SURELY.

IT WOULD SEEM THIS JANET JONES, FINE'S COMMON-LAW WIFE, EXERTED SUCH A CONTROLLING *FORCE* ON HIM THAT I BELIEVE HE CREATED THIS *DARKER* PERSONA, THIS "*BRAINIAC*" EMERGED, TO REGAIN CONTROL OF HIS LIFE.

IT IS MY FIRM BELIEF, DETECTIVE, THAT MILTON FINE COULD NOT HAVE KILLED THOSE DERELICTS...

BUT THIS *BRAINIAC* COULD HAVE.

I'M ALMOST MORE INCLINED TO BELIEVE THE STORY *FINE* TOLD-- ABOUT *ALIENS* INVADING HIS *MIND*.

EXCUSE ME, BUT DOES FINE HAVE ANY LIVING RELATIVES? SOMEONE I COULD TALK TO?

APPARENTLY, MS. JONES HAD A SON, BUT WE DON'T KNOW HIS WHEREABOUTS.

OH, ONE OTHER THING TO KNOW... MILTON FINE WAS SUBJECTED TO A BATTERY OF MENTAL AND PHYSICAL EXAMS IN OUR CARE...

THE DAY HE *GOT AWAY* FROM US-- AT HIS ASSISTANT'S FUNERAL--

--HE WAS DIAGNOSED AS HAVING A *BRAIN TUMOR*... WHAT WE FEEL IS THE ORIGIN OF HIS HEADACHES.

"I DON'T KNOW WHY EVERYBODY'S BEEN ON MY CASE LATELY..."

"I KNOW I'VE GOT PROBLEMS..."

"ER...UM...WHAT TIME IS IT?..."

SEVEN-FIFTEEN.

DRINKING ISN'T A PROBLEM. IT'S A SOLUTION. IT HELPS ME TO IDENTIFY WHAT'S REALLY WRONG IN MY LIFE.

SURE, LADY.

I MEAN, I'M STILL NEW AROUND HERE--I'M FROM CALIFORNIA, ORIGINALLY.

LOIS HATES ME. PERRY WON'T UNDERSTAND ME. CLARK IS HARD TO GET THROUGH TO. JIMMY...

HEY! DAVE! WAKE UP! THIS IS A RESPECTABLE BAR NOW!

...NOW JIMMY--HE'S SO CUTE IN HIS BOWTIES. SO SQUARE--HE THINKS THE WORLD OF ME--BUT HE'S STILL A KID.

LOOK, MISS, I DON'T--

...OH, HE'S GREAT WITH MY SON ADAM--DID I MENTION I HAD A SON?

I SHARE CUSTODY WITH ADAM'S FATHER. YOU KNOW, I HADN'T EVEN SEEN MY SON SINCE HE WAS JUST A BABY...

WELL, I NEVER CONTESTED THE COURT RULING BACK THEN-- I WAS TOO BUSY--NOW I GET TO BE A MOM SIX MONTHS A YEAR...

...BUT I'M NO GOOD AT IT--I DON'T KNOW HOW.--HE'S USED TO NICE THINGS--AND I WANT HIM TO LOVE ME AS MUCH AS HIS DADDY...

IT'S JUST SO DIFFICULT-- TWENTY-FOUR HOURS A DAY-- IF IT WEREN'T FOR JIMMY-- DID I MENTION JIMMY...?

UH-HUH!

HE'S SO GOOD WITH ADAM--TAKING HIM PLACES--HE'S BEEN SO GOOD. YOU CAN'T REALIZE...

I THINK YOU HAVE HAD ENOUGH FOR ONE NIGHT. WANT ME TO GET YOU A CAB?

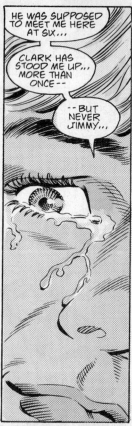

HE WAS SUPPOSED TO MEET ME HERE AT SIX...

CLARK HAS STOOD ME UP... MORE THAN ONCE--

--BUT NEVER JIMMY...

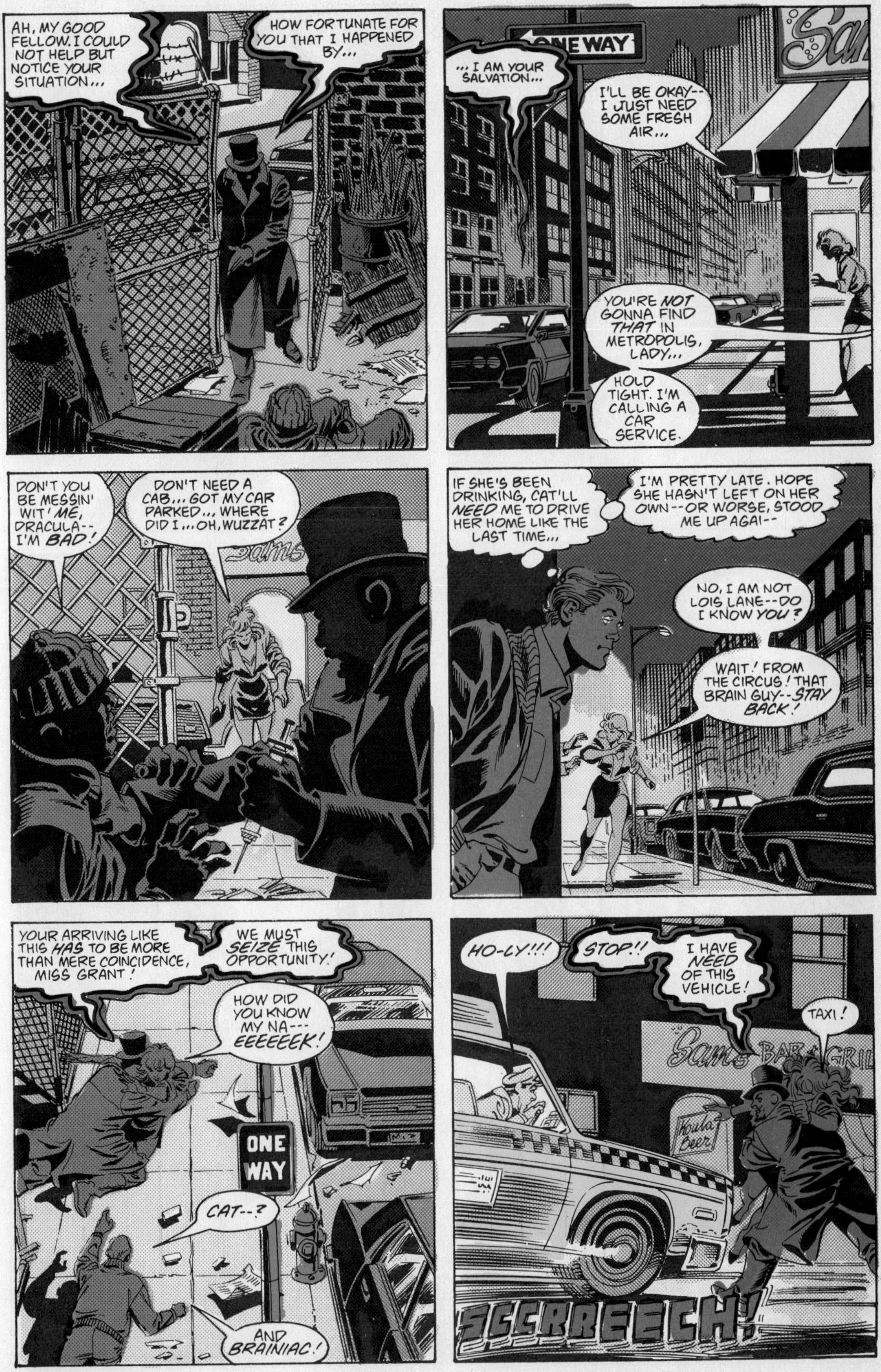
AH, MY GOOD FELLOW. I COULD NOT HELP BUT NOTICE YOUR SITUATION...
HOW FORTUNATE FOR YOU THAT I HAPPENED BY...
ONE WAY
...I AM YOUR SALVATION...
I'LL BE OKAY-- I JUST NEED SOME FRESH AIR...
YOU'RE NOT GONNA FIND THAT IN METROPOLIS, LADY...
HOLD TIGHT. I'M CALLING A CAR SERVICE.
DON'T YOU BE MESSIN' WIT' ME, DRACULA-- I'M BAD!
DON'T NEED A CAB... GOT MY CAR PARKED... WHERE DID I... OH, WUZZAT?
IF SHE'S BEEN DRINKING, CAT'LL NEED ME TO DRIVE HER HOME LIKE THE LAST TIME...
I'M PRETTY LATE. HOPE SHE HASN'T LEFT ON HER OWN--OR WORSE, STOOD ME UP AGAI--
NO, I AM NOT LOIS LANE--DO I KNOW YOU?
WAIT! FROM THE CIRCUS! THAT BRAIN GUY--STAY BACK!
YOUR ARRIVING LIKE THIS HAS TO BE MORE THAN MERE COINCIDENCE, MISS GRANT!
WE MUST SEIZE THIS OPPORTUNITY!
HOW DID YOU KNOW MY NA--- EEEEEEK!
ONE WAY
CAT--?
AND BRAINIAC!
HO-LY!!!
STOP!!
I HAVE NEED OF THIS VEHICLE!
TAXI!
SCCRREECH!

THE LADY HAS HAD *TOO* MUCH TO DRINK!

YOU BEEN TO A COSTUME PARTY?

JUST *DRIVE,* YOU FOOL!

YES, I WILL *DRIVE.*

THEY'RE GETTING AWAY!

HEY! STOP!!

DARN! NO USE!

NEED A CAB, BUD?

MY FARE JUST *STIFFED* ME.

CAN YOU CATCH UP TO THAT CAB THAT JUST *LEFT?*

THAT GUY *STEAL* YER GIRL?

SOMETHING LIKE THAT.

IT'S BEEN FIFTEEN MINUTES SINCE I SIGNALED SUPERMAN WITH MY WATCH...

ZEEEEEEEEEEE

...THIS IS *NOT* A NEIGHBORHOOD I WANT TO BE STRANDED IN!

SUPERMAN MUST BE OUT OF RANGE OF THE SIGNAL...

THE CABBIE TOLD HIS DISPATCHER TO GET THE POLICE, BUT CAT MAY NOT HAVE THAT LONG TO WAIT.

KATHOOOM

WE'VE BEEN *SNOOPING,* HAVEN'T WE, YOUNG SIR?

ULP!

I *DOUBT* many psychiatrists would say that it's *THERAPEUTIC* to sit in a room and stare into space all day...!

...BUT somehow it's made it a *LITTLE* easier for me to deal with my actions in that alternate world. *

*SUPERMAN #22.

BEST thing for me to do *NOW* is throw myself *BACK* into the thick of it and not let my detractors, like Morgan Edge, under my skin!

SEEMS THE *BIG APRICOT* SURVIVED MY ABSENCE!

FORREST FOR PRESIDENT
BETTER THAN THE REST

I have no doubt Edge will be expounding on that very subject as soon as he--

ARRRGH!

EEEEEEEEEEEEE

JIMMY OLSEN'S SIGNAL WATCH... *DEAFENING*...

...AMPLIFIED-- SO *LOUD*...MY HEAD--LOSING CONTROL...

KROCK-KK

SCRATCH ONE CHIMNEY...

LUCKILY, THE DEBRIS IS CONFINED TO THE ROOF. THANK GOD NO ONE'S HURT BELOW...

THE SOUND IS EASING UP...

...ENOUGH FOR ME TO FOLLOW IT...

119

EEEEEEEEEEEEEEEEEEEEEEEEEEEEEEEEEEEEE

"HELP ME, SUPERMAN! SAVE ME, SUPERMAN!" *PITIFUL!*

WE HAVE BEEN AWAITING YOU, MAN OF STEEL.

IT TOOK SOME TIME, BUT ONCE I HOMED IN ON YOUR RATHER DISTINCT BRAINWAVES IT WAS CHILD'S PLAY TO LEAD YOU HERE--

--BY MENTALLY MANIPULATING YOUR MIND TO *BELIEVE* THE SIGNAL BEACON HAD BEEN INCREASED!

BRAKOOOM!

MILTON FINE!

MILTON FINE DOES NOT RESIDE HERE ANYMORE!

MY NAME IS VRIL DOX... BUT YOU MAY ADDRESS ME AS *BRAINIAC!*

AND AS TO WHY I'VE SUMMONED YOU... CHANCING UPON YOUR COMPANIONS SERVED TO REMIND ME OF *OUR* UNFINISHED BUSINESS!

"OUR" BUSINESS WAS CONCLUDED WHEN I TOOK YOU TO THE *HOSPITAL*..

LISTEN.... I'M WILLING TO TALK, IF YOU LET *THEM* GO FREE FIRST.

OUT OF THE QUESTION... THESE TWO ARE TO BE TEST SUBJECTS FOR MY EXPERIMENTS--

--AS I SEARCH FOR THE ORGANIC SERUM I NEED TO STAVE OFF THIS BODY'S REJECTION OF MY ALIEN ESSENCE!

STOP! YOU'RE INSANE!

HAVE YOU SO SOON FORGOTTEN-- *THIS?*

FWAAAM!

BWA-TASH

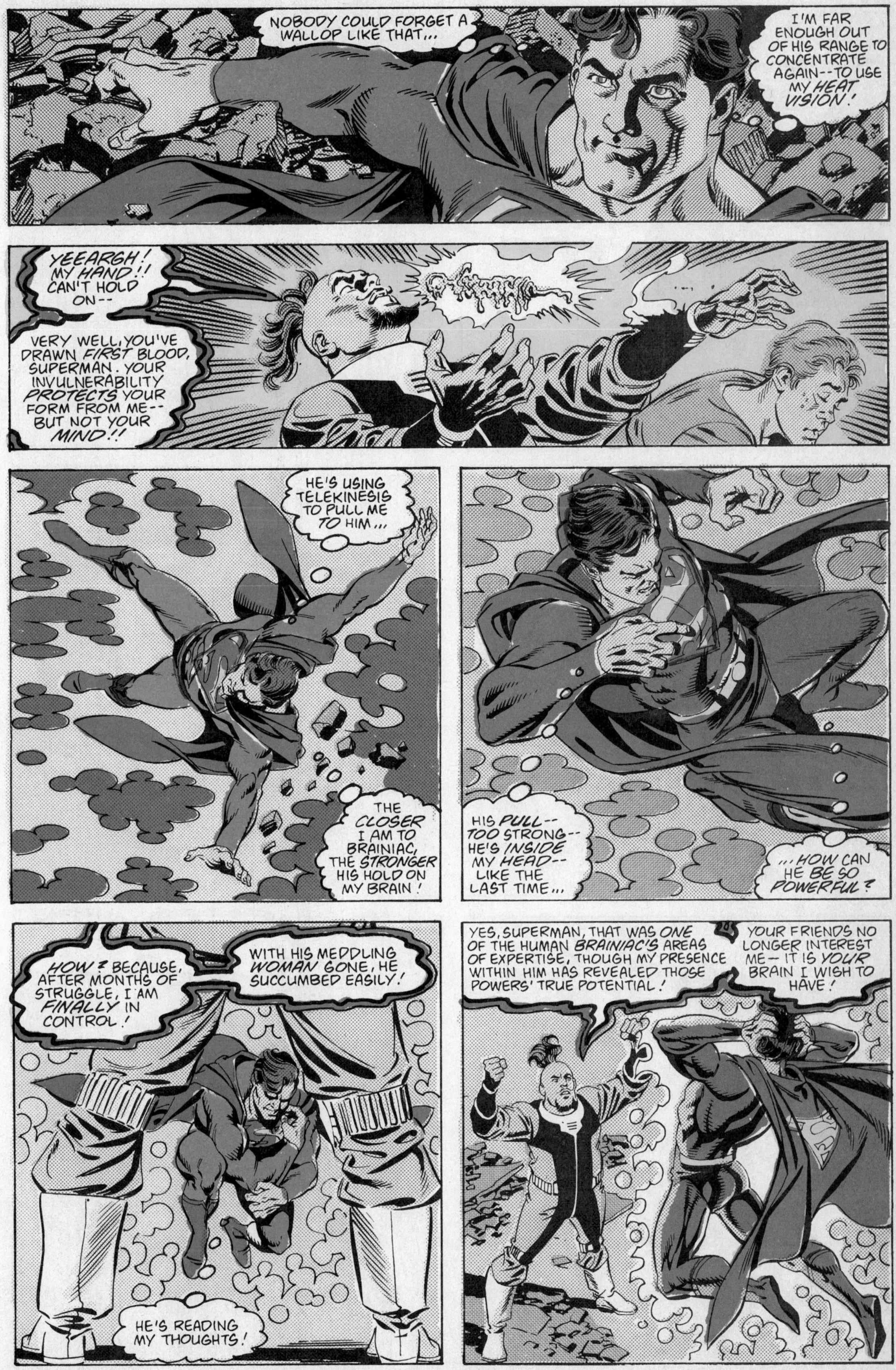
NOBODY COULD FORGET A WALLOP LIKE THAT...
I'M FAR ENOUGH OUT OF HIS RANGE TO CONCENTRATE AGAIN--TO USE MY HEAT VISION!
YEEARGH! MY HAND!! CAN'T HOLD ON--
VERY WELL, YOU'VE DRAWN FIRST BLOOD, SUPERMAN. YOUR INVULNERABILITY PROTECTS YOUR FORM FROM ME--BUT NOT YOUR MIND!!
HE'S USING TELEKINESIS TO PULL ME TO HIM...
THE CLOSER I AM TO BRAINIAC, THE STRONGER HIS HOLD ON MY BRAIN!
HIS PULL--TOO STRONG--HE'S INSIDE MY HEAD--LIKE THE LAST TIME...
...HOW CAN HE BE SO POWERFUL?
HOW? BECAUSE, AFTER MONTHS OF STRUGGLE, I AM FINALLY IN CONTROL!
WITH HIS MEDDLING WOMAN GONE, HE SUCCUMBED EASILY!
HE'S READING MY THOUGHTS!
YES, SUPERMAN, THAT WAS ONE OF THE HUMAN BRAINIAC'S AREAS OF EXPERTISE, THOUGH MY PRESENCE WITHIN HIM HAS REVEALED THOSE POWERS' TRUE POTENTIAL!
YOUR FRIENDS NO LONGER INTEREST ME--IT IS YOUR BRAIN I WISH TO HAVE!

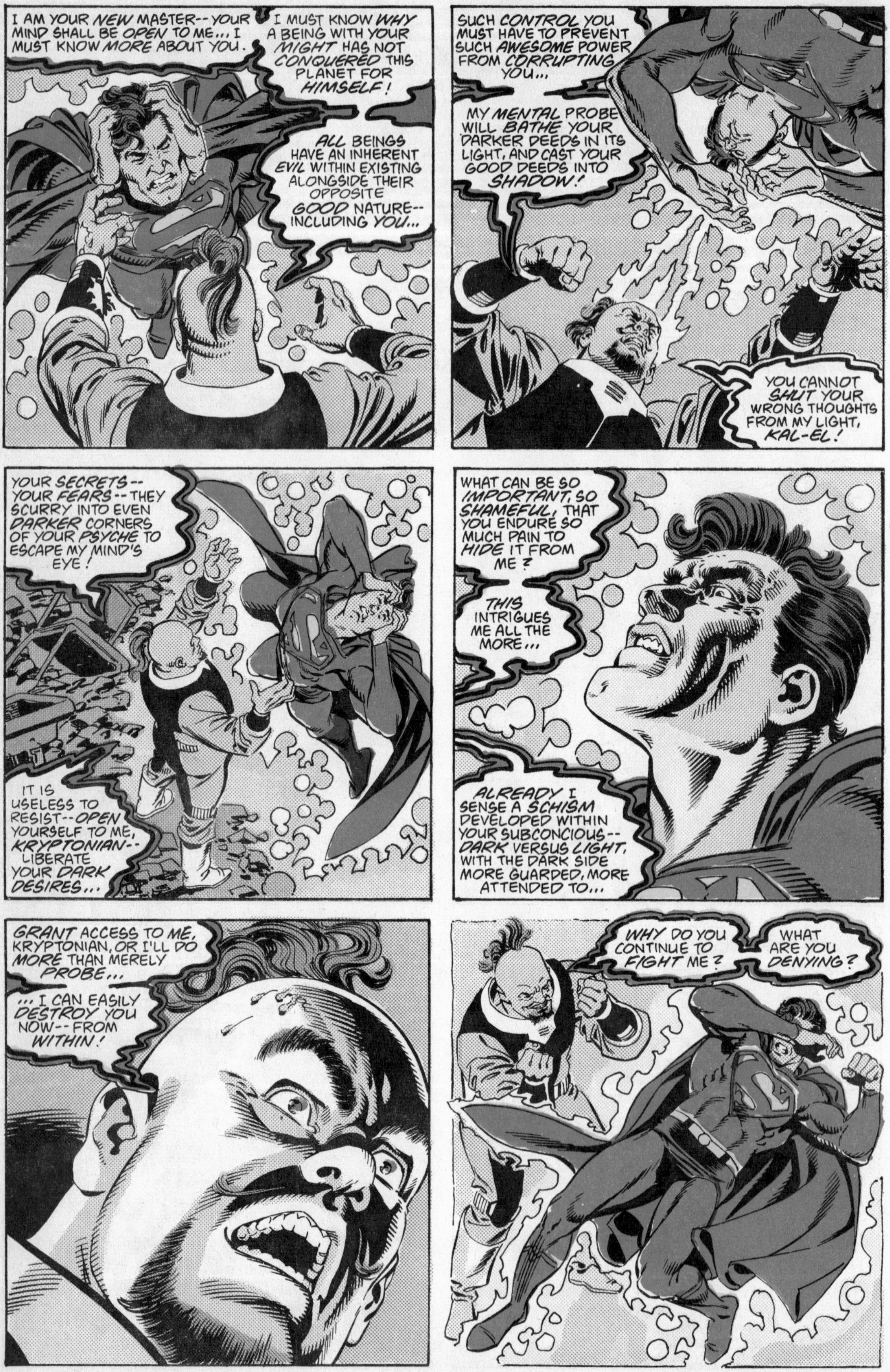
I AM YOUR NEW MASTER--YOUR MIND SHALL BE OPEN TO ME... I MUST KNOW MORE ABOUT YOU.
I MUST KNOW WHY A BEING WITH YOUR MIGHT HAS NOT CONQUERED THIS PLANET FOR HIMSELF!
ALL BEINGS HAVE AN INHERENT EVIL WITHIN EXISTING ALONGSIDE THEIR OPPOSITE GOOD NATURE--INCLUDING YOU...
SUCH CONTROL YOU MUST HAVE TO PREVENT SUCH AWESOME POWER FROM CORRUPTING YOU...
MY MENTAL PROBE WILL BATHE YOUR DARKER DEEDS IN ITS LIGHT, AND CAST YOUR GOOD DEEDS INTO SHADOW!
YOU CANNOT SHUT YOUR WRONG THOUGHTS FROM MY LIGHT, KAL-EL!
YOUR SECRETS--YOUR FEARS--THEY SCURRY INTO EVEN DARKER CORNERS OF YOUR PSYCHE TO ESCAPE MY MIND'S EYE!
IT IS USELESS TO RESIST--OPEN YOURSELF TO ME, KRYPTONIAN--LIBERATE YOUR DARK DESIRES...
WHAT CAN BE SO IMPORTANT, SO SHAMEFUL, THAT YOU ENDURE SO MUCH PAIN TO HIDE IT FROM ME?
THIS INTRIGUES ME ALL THE MORE...
ALREADY I SENSE A SCHISM DEVELOPED WITHIN YOUR SUBCONCIOUS--DARK VERSUS LIGHT, WITH THE DARK SIDE MORE GUARDED, MORE ATTENDED TO...
GRANT ACCESS TO ME, KRYPTONIAN, OR I'LL DO MORE THAN MERELY PROBE...
...I CAN EASILY DESTROY YOU NOW--FROM WITHIN!
WHY DO YOU CONTINUE TO FIGHT ME?
WHAT ARE YOU DENYING?

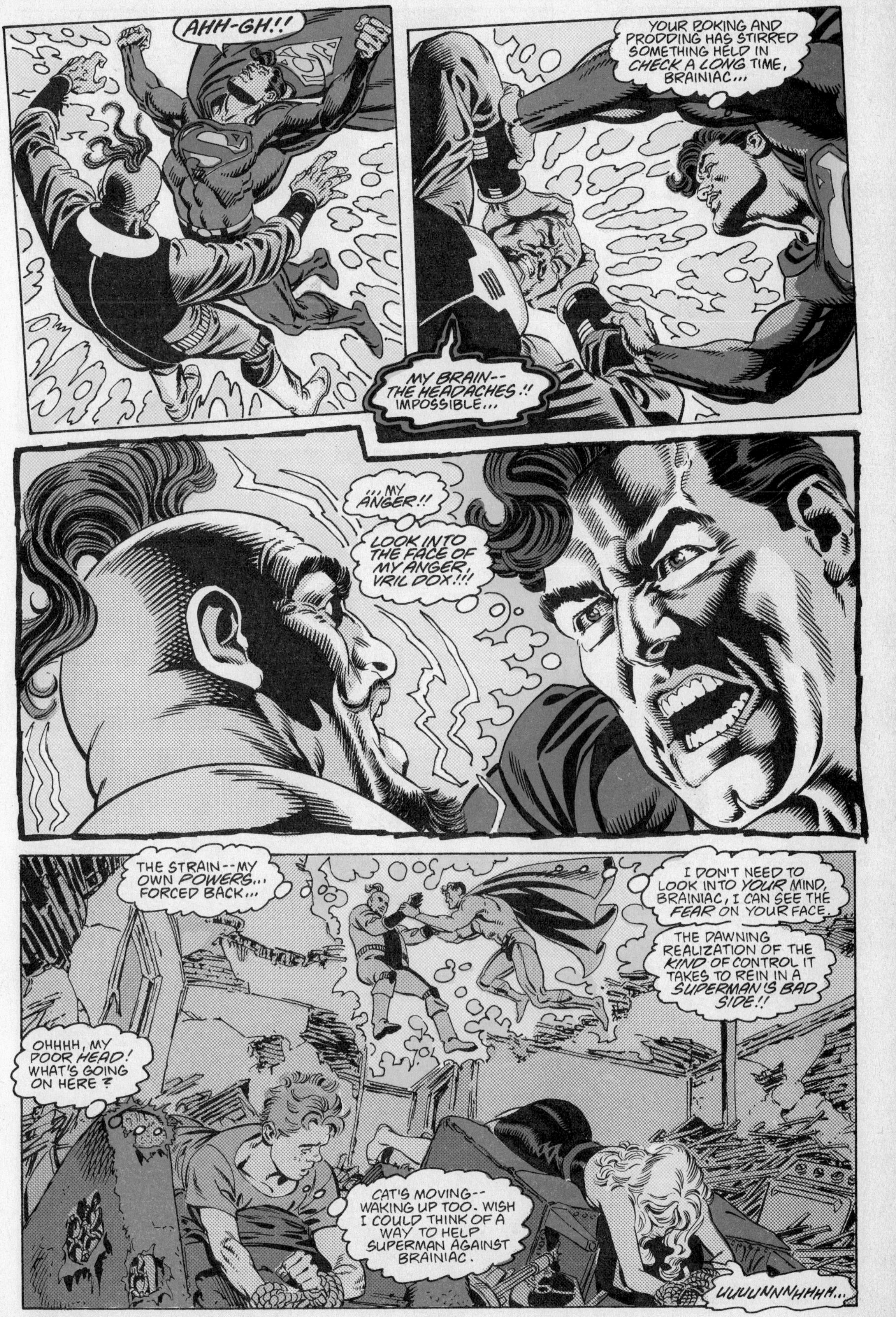
AHH-GH!!
YOUR POKING AND PRODDING HAS STIRRED SOMETHING HELD IN CHECK A LONG TIME, BRAINIAC...
MY BRAIN-- THE HEADACHES!! IMPOSSIBLE...
...MY ANGER!!
LOOK INTO THE FACE OF MY ANGER, VRIL DOX!!!
THE STRAIN--MY OWN POWERS... FORCED BACK...
I DON'T NEED TO LOOK INTO YOUR MIND, BRAINIAC, I CAN SEE THE FEAR ON YOUR FACE.
THE DAWNING REALIZATION OF THE KIND OF CONTROL IT TAKES TO REIN IN A SUPERMAN'S BAD SIDE!!
OHHHH, MY POOR HEAD! WHAT'S GOING ON HERE?
CAT'S MOVING-- WAKING UP TOO. WISH I COULD THINK OF A WAY TO HELP SUPERMAN AGAINST BRAINIAC.
UUUUNNHHHH...

THEY BOTH SEEM TO BE JUST *STANDING* THERE... NOT EVEN MAKING A *SOUND*...

...BUT THAT SWIRLING LIGHT-SHOW SURROUNDING THEM IS SPEAKING *VOLUMES* TO ME!

I'D BETTER GET CAT OUTSIDE QUICKLY...

I'VE NEVER SEEN SUPERMAN SO *MAD*... HE LOOKS DOWN RIGHT *EVIL!* HE LOOKS AS IF HE COULD *KILL* SOMEBODY!

AWWW, HE DOESN'T *NEED* ME... IT LOOKS LIKE HE'S FINALLY GAINING THE EDGE OVER BRAINIAC--

--AND I DON'T WANNA BE HERE IF HE DOES TOTALLY *LOSE IT* ANYWAY!

HOLD YOUR FIRE! THAT'S *JIMMY OLSEN*... AND...

LOOKS LIKE YOU GOT YOUR BUTT OUT OF THERE JUST IN TIME, *JUNIOR!*

ANYONE ELSE IN THERE BESIDES YOU AND YOUR GIRLFRIEND?

ONLY SUPERMAN AND BRAINIAC, I THINK...

I MEAN SUPERMAN AND MILTON--

--FINE!

YOU DID IT, SUPERMAN! YOU STOPPED BRAINIAC, BUT HOW? WHAT HAPPENED?

SUPERMAN?

WHAT KIND OF EXPLOSION WAS THAT? NO BURNS ON HIS BODY...

I THINK CAT'S GOING TO BE OKAY...

GUESS THINGS TURNED OUT. YOU SAVED THE DAY!

DOX-- IS HE...

NAHHH. HE'S ALIVE. PRETTY BUSTED UP, BUT HE'LL LIVE.

YOU COULD'VE KILLED HIM!

WHAT?

EASE UP, PAL! SUPERMAN'S NO KILLER!

THAT'S NOT WHAT I MEANT.

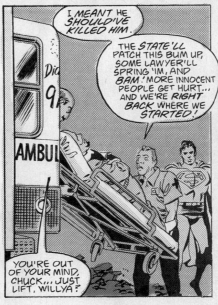

I MEANT HE SHOULD'VE KILLED HIM.

THE STATE'LL PATCH THIS BUM UP, SOME LAWYER'LL SPRING 'IM, AND BAM! MORE INNOCENT PEOPLE GET HURT... AND WE'RE RIGHT BACK WHERE WE STARTED!

YOU'RE OUT OF YOUR MIND, CHUCK.... JUST LIFT, WILLYA?

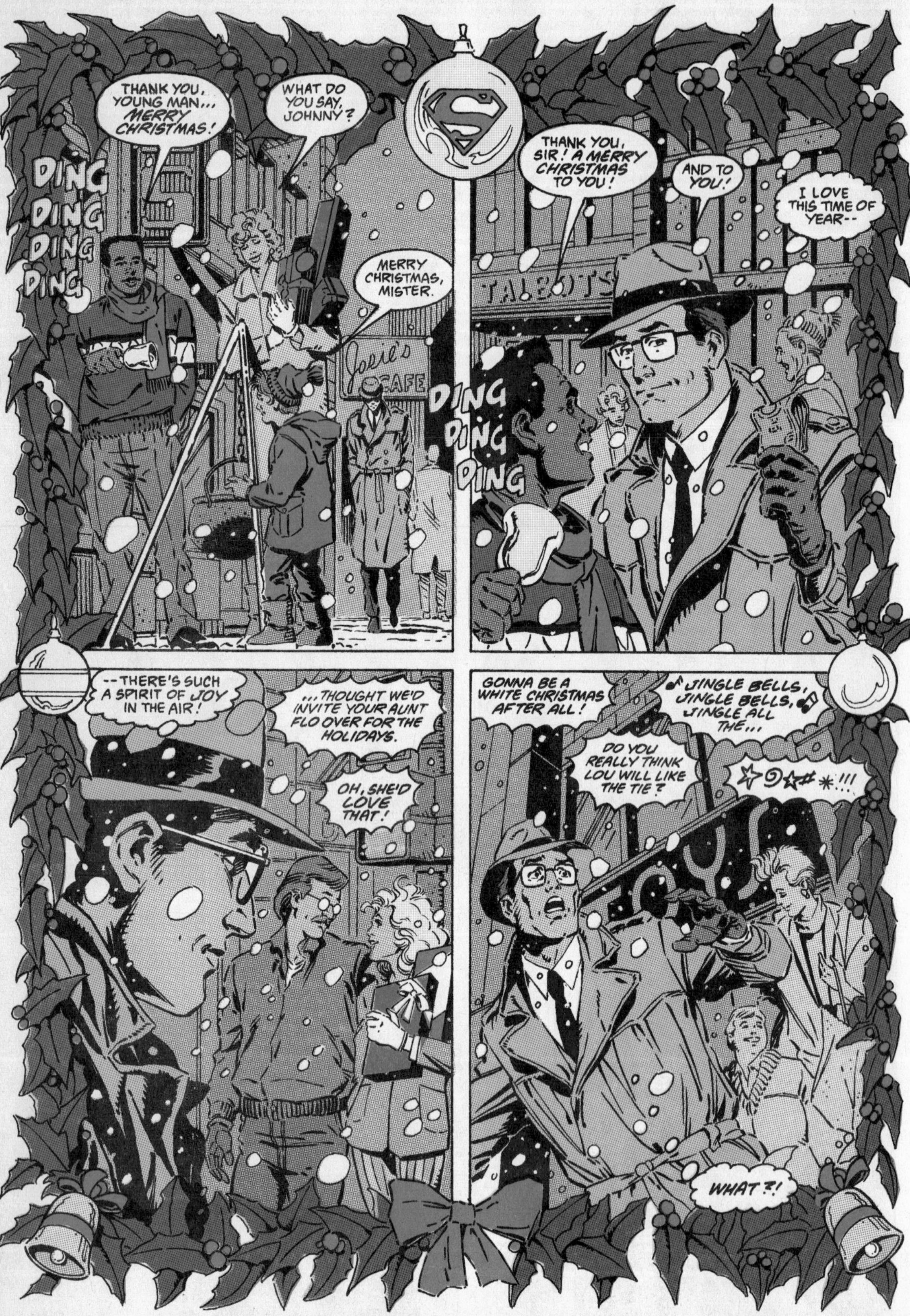
THANK YOU, YOUNG MAN... MERRY CHRISTMAS!
WHAT DO YOU SAY, JOHNNY?
DING DING DING DING
MERRY CHRISTMAS, MISTER.
Josie's CAFE
TALBOTS
DING DING DING
THANK YOU, SIR! A MERRY CHRISTMAS TO YOU!
AND TO YOU!
I LOVE THIS TIME OF YEAR--
--THERE'S SUCH A SPIRIT OF JOY IN THE AIR!
...THOUGHT WE'D INVITE YOUR AUNT FLO OVER FOR THE HOLIDAYS.
OH, SHE'D LOVE THAT!
GONNA BE A WHITE CHRISTMAS AFTER ALL!
JINGLE BELLS, JINGLE BELLS, JINGLE ALL THE...
DO YOU REALLY THINK LOU WILL LIKE THE TIE?
WHAT?!

I DON'T BELIEVE THIS....

SOMEBODY IS DEFINITELY *NOT* INTO THE SPIRIT OF THINGS!

FROM THE SOUND OF THINGS, THE PROBLEM IS ABOUT SIX BLOCKS AWAY...

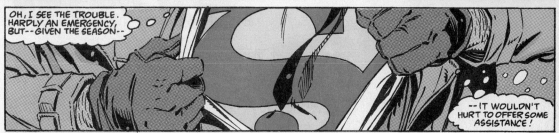

OH, I SEE THE TROUBLE. HARDLY AN EMERGENCY, BUT--GIVEN THE SEASON--

--IT WOULDN'T HURT TO OFFER SOME ASSISTANCE!

...I JUST *DO NOT* BELIEVE THIS! WE HAVE ONLY TWO FLOORS TO GO! YOU'RE *SURE* YOU CAN'T FIX IT?

SORRY, JER--

LUXURY CONDO
AVAILABLE SPRING

--BUT THE ENGINE'S *SHOT*! I'LL HAVE TO LOWER THE LOAD BACK DOWN AND SEND FOR A REPLACEMENT.

THERE GO OUR *BONUSES*! WE'LL *NEVER* FINISH BEFORE CHRISTMAS NOW.

EXCUSE ME, MAY I GIVE YOU MEN A HAND?

HOLY GEEZ...

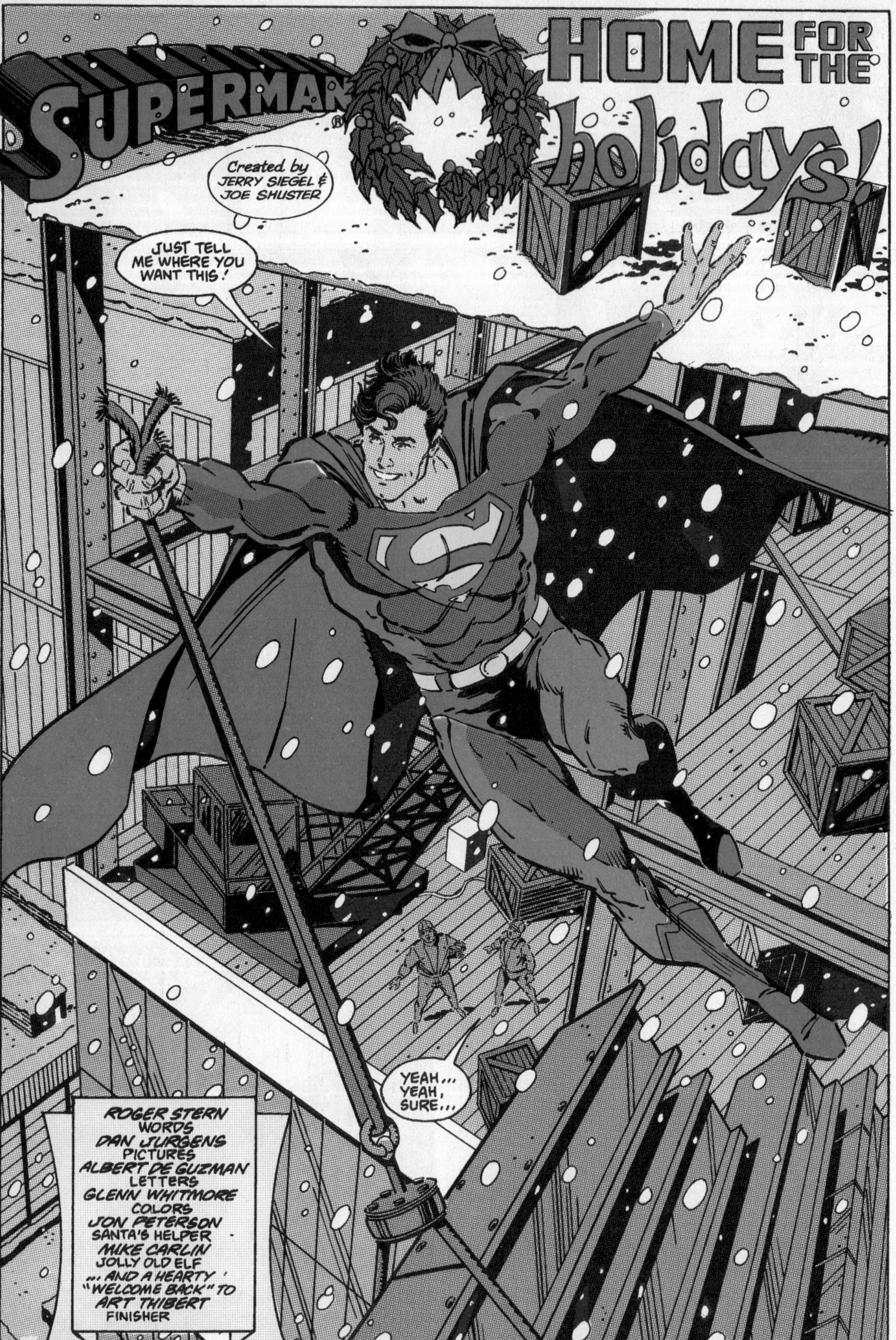
SUPERMAN®
HOME FOR THE holidays!
Created by JERRY SIEGEL & JOE SHUSTER
JUST TELL ME WHERE YOU WANT THIS!
YEAH... YEAH, SURE...
ROGER STERN WORDS
DAN JURGENS PICTURES
ALBERT DE GUZMAN LETTERS
GLENN WHITMORE COLORS
JON PETERSON SANTA'S HELPER
MIKE CARLIN JOLLY OLD ELF
...AND A HEARTY "WELCOME BACK" TO ART THIBERT FINISHER

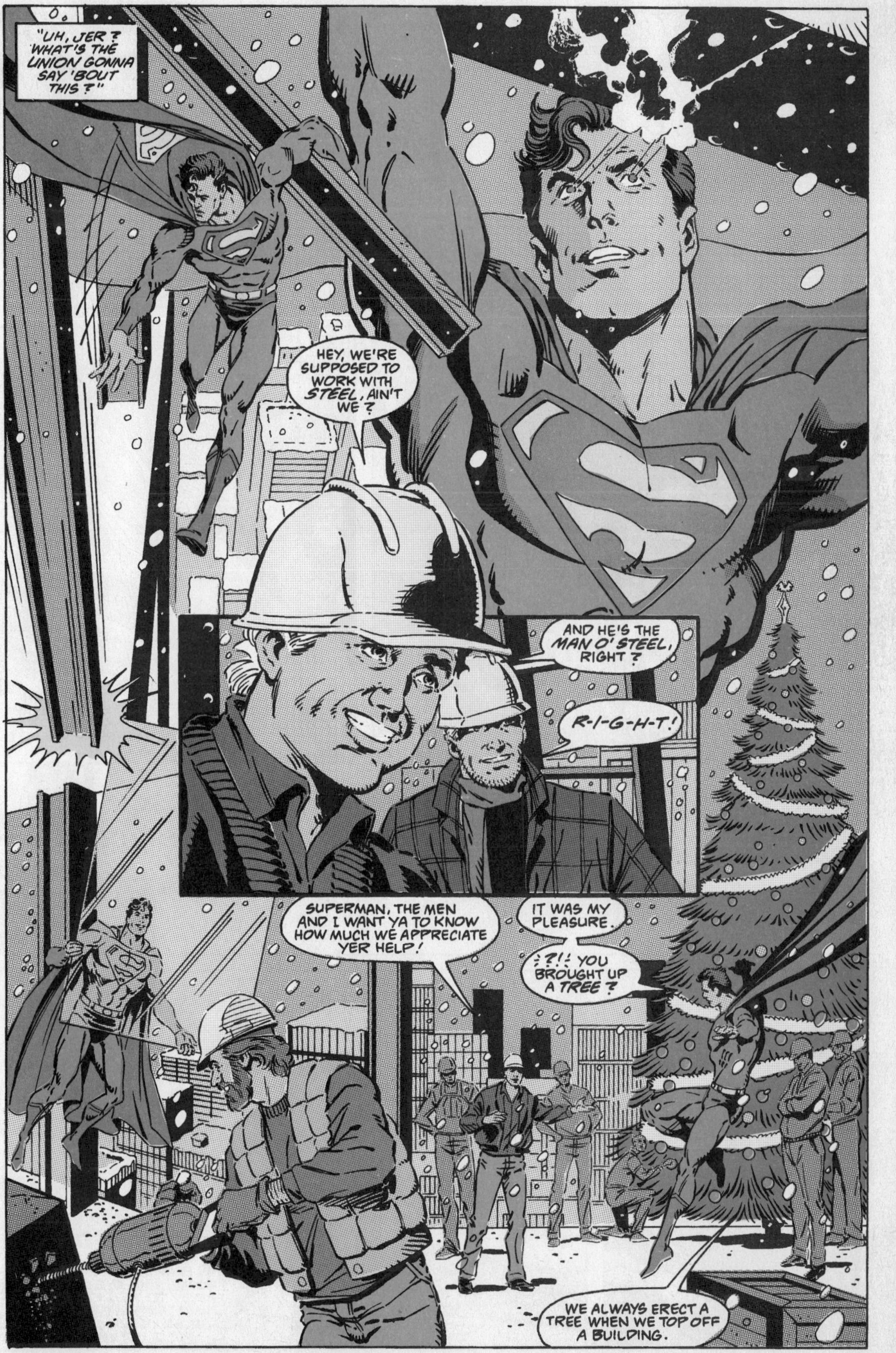
"UH, JER? WHAT'S THE UNION GONNA SAY 'BOUT THIS?"
HEY, WE'RE SUPPOSED TO WORK WITH STEEL, AIN'T WE?
AND HE'S THE MAN O' STEEL, RIGHT?
R-I-G-H-T!
SUPERMAN, THE MEN AND I WANT YA TO KNOW HOW MUCH WE APPRECIATE YER HELP!
IT WAS MY PLEASURE.
?!! YOU BROUGHT UP A TREE?
WE ALWAYS ERECT A TREE WHEN WE TOP OFF A BUILDING.

YEAH, IT'S AN OLD CUSTOM.

CARE TO JOIN US FOR SANDWICHES AN' COFFEE?

THANKS, I WISH I COULD, BUT I HAVE OTHER COMMITMENTS.

AIN'T SURPRISIN', A BUSY GUY LIKE YOU! HAVE YOURSELF A GOOD ONE, Y'HEAR?

♪ GOD REST YE MERRY, GENTLEMEN... LET NOTHING YOU DISMAY! ♪

THAT FELT GOOD....

...BUT IT SERIOUSLY CUT INTO MY MORNING.

I'D BETTER RETRIEVE MY HAT AND COAT FROM WHERE I LEFT THEM--

--AND STEP ON IT!

IT WOULDN'T DO TO BE LATE FOR MY LAST DAY AT THE PLANET!

MY LAST DAY... HARD TO BELIEVE THAT I WON'T BE WORKING HERE ANYMORE.

THE PEOPLE HERE HAVE BECOME LIKE A SECOND FAMILY TO ME... PERRY, JIMMY, LOIS... EVEN CAT GRANT IN HER OWN PECULIAR WAY.

BUT WHEN CAREER OPPORTUNITIES BECKON, YOU CAN'T IGNORE THEM.

I COULDN'T VERY WELL--

--PASS UP COLLIN THORNTON'S OFFER--

-- TO BECOME MANAGING EDITOR--

--OF NEWSTIME!

COULD I?

STILL, THE *PLANET'S* BEEN A BIG PART OF MY LIFE, THESE PAST FEW YEARS. I'M GOING TO *MISS* THIS CREW...

GOOD MORNING, ALL!

ANYBODY?

HELLO? CHARLIE? DAVE?

WHY ARE THEY ALL GIVING ME THE COLD SHOULDER? BECAUSE I'M LEAVING?! I WOULDN'T HAVE THOUGHT--!

KENT! JUST THE MAN I'M LOOKING FOR!

LOIS, *HI!* NEW HAIR STYLE?

UH-HUH. THIS IS FOR YOU!

OH, YOU DIDN'T HAVE TO--!

HEY, THIS IS AN *EMPTY* BOX!

WELL, YOU *ARE* CLEANING OUT YOUR DESK TODAY, AREN'T YOU?

...SOME OF US STILL HAVE *WORK* TO DO.

EXCUSE ME...

OVER 1600 MILES DUE WEST, ANOTHER KIND OF WORK PROCEEDS WITHIN A REMOTE ROCKY MOUNTAIN RESEARCH CENTER.

AND THOUGH THIS FACILITY IS SECRETLY OWNED BY INDUSTRIALIST LEX LUTHOR--

--THE WORK CURRENTLY UNDER WAY IS NOT TO HIS LIKING!

PUT--ME-- DOWN!

IT'S UPSETTING TO BE SO HELPLESS... ISN'T IT, LEX? I FELT MUCH THE SAME WAY--

--BEFORE I FREED MY MIND FROM THE BODY YOU HAD KEPT DRUGGED. BUT, LOOK AT ME NOW!

AND LOOK AT YOU! HAH-HA!

GO AHEAD, BRAINIAC, GLOAT WHILE YOU CAN! MY DISAPPEARANCE WILL NOT GO UNNOTICED-- MY STAFF WILL LAUNCH A WORLDWIDE SEARCH FOR ME!

I THINK NOT.

YOU FORGET, LEX--

--I CONTROL DR. HAPPERSEN HERE--AND THROUGH HIM YOUR ENTIRE COMMUNICATIONS NETWORK!

"THE TWO OF US HAVE CREATED A QUITE CONVINCING COMPUTER-GENERATED IMAGE OF YOURSELF. IN FACT, AT THIS VERY MOMENT, 'YOU' ARE BROADCASTING SOME MOST WELCOME NEWS--

"--TO YOUR HOME OFFICE IN METROPOLIS."

I'LL BE SPENDING THE NEXT MONTH IN THE ISLANDS. ISSUE HOLIDAY BONUSES FOR ALL EMPLOYEES, EQUAL TO ONE-HALF EACH PERSON'S PROFIT-SHARING BENEFIT FOR THE YEAR.

SEASONS GREETINGS, ALL!

MR. L-- THANKS TO YOU...

"...THIS WILL BE A CHRISTMAS TO REMEMBER!"

CLARK KENT

WOW... I WAS ISSUED THIS NAMEPLATE THE FIRST WEEK I CAME TO WORK AT THE *PLANET*.

IT'S OUTLASTED FOUR STAPLERS, THREE COFFEE MUGS, AND A TAPE DISPENSER. GUESS I SHOULD TAKE IT WITH ME...

...IT WON'T BE OF USE TO ANYONE HERE... UNLESS THEY HIRE A REPORTER WITH THE SAME NAME.

I FOUGHT A LOT OF DEADLINES IN THIS ROOM, BUT I WASN'T ALONE IN THAT. THERE WERE PLENTY OF *GOOD TIMES*, TOO... A LOT OF *GOOD PEOPLE*...

HEY, JULIE... MORT! WHAT DO YOU SAY WE HIT ENRICO'S FOR LUNCH? MY TREAT!

SORRY, KENT.

BUSY.

SO MUCH FOR CAMARADERIE!

KENT! MY OFFICE -- NOW!

UH, SURE, CHIEF... BE RIGHT THERE.

KENT, I'VE NEVER MINCED WORDS WITH YOU BEFORE, AND I HAVE NO INTENTION OF STARTING NOW.

YES, SIR.

THE EDITOR'S JOB AT *NEWSTIME* IS A PLUM -- I WON'T DENY THAT. THE *PLANET* HAS NOTHING TO MATCH THE CHALLENGES YOU'LL FIND THERE... AND PROBABLY WON'T UNTIL *I* RETIRE.

BEING AN EDITOR ISN'T THE SAME AS BEING A REPORTER OR A COLUMNIST.

I THINK I CAN HANDLE IT.

I *KNOW* YOU CAN. THAT'S NOT THE POINT.

I WAS WHERE YOU ARE ONCE... I GAVE UP REPORTING TO SIT BEHIND A DESK. I'VE NEVER FORGOTTEN WHAT IT'S LIKE TO CHASE DOWN A STORY--AND NOT A DAY'S PASSED THAT I HAVEN'T MISSED IT.

YOU'RE A GOOD NEWSPAPERMAN, KENT--YOU'LL DO *FINE!* JUST TRUST IN YOUR INSTINCTS.... AND *ALWAYS* LISTEN TO YOUR PEOPLE.

AND IF YOU EVER NEED ADVICE, FOR GOD'S SAKE, DON'T THINK OF ME AS A COMPETITOR.

I WON'T, PERRY. THANKS.

AND IF YOU EVER COME TO YOUR SENSES AND RETURN TO REPORTING, I'LL SKIN YOU ALIVE IF YOU DON'T CALL ME FIRST. IS THAT CLEAR?

AS A BELL, CHIEF!

IN THAT CASE, I THINK THESE PEOPLE HAVE SOMETHING TO SAY!

HANH?!

GOOD LUCK, CLARK

SURPRISE!!

THE COLD SHOULDERS, THE SILENT TREATMENT.... IT WAS ALL A *PUT-ON!*

WHAT ELSE?

I'M GOING TO MISS YOU, CLARK. YOU'RE THE BEST COMPETITION A REPORTER EVER HAD!

WE'RE ALL GOING TO MISS YOU, CLARKIE! LOADS AND *LOADS!*

CAT....

...GONNA MISS YA.

WHIT? THANKS.

IN ALL THE YEARS I'VE WORKED HERE, I'VE *NEVER* HEARD YOU SAY MORE THAN TWO WORDS IN A ROW. I FEEL ...*HONORED!*

I DON'T KNOW WHAT TO SAY, BUT--!

CHOKIN' UP. 'BYE.

GOOD-BYE, WHIT. MERRY CHRISTMAS.

HI, EVERYBODY! AM I TOO LATE?

WELL, OLSEN, YOU MISSED THE BIG MOMENT OF SURPRISE, BUT NOT BY MUCH. WELCOME BACK, SON!

COME IN, JIMMY. IT'S GOOD TO HAVE YOU BACK!

IT'S GOOD TO BE BACK, MISS LANE.

YOU WERE OUT SO LONG, YOU REALLY HAD US WORRIED!

HEY, I'M OKAY! I'VE GOTTEN A CLEAN BILL OF HEALTH, AND MY HAIR'S ALL GROWN BACK IN...

...MOSTLY.

YOU LOOK GREAT, JIM.

THANKS, MR. KENT. BUT, GOSH, I STILL CAN'T BELIEVE YOU'RE LEAVING! I ALMOST DROPPED THE PHONE WHEN ALICE CALLED TO TELL ME.

IT WON'T BE THE SAME HERE WITHOUT YOU.

JIMMY'S RIGHT. ALICE ORGANIZED THIS PARTY, BUT ALL OF US WANTED YOU TO KNOW THAT....THAT...

135

HERE NOW! KENT'S NOT GOING *OVERSEAS*-- HE'S JUST MOVING ACROSS TOWN! AND THIS IS *STILL* THE NATION'S GREATEST NEWSPAPER!

I'M NOT GOING TO LET ANYONE OF YOU REST ON YOUR LAURELS! I HOPE *YOU'RE* READY TO GET BACK TO WORK, OLSEN!

GOSH, YES, CHIEF!

THAT'S TELLING THEM, PERRY!

I NEVER MEANT THAT THE PAPER WOULD FALL APART...

...IT'S JUST THAT, WITH MR. KENT LEAVING, IT'S LIKE THE END OF AN *ERA!*

SIGH THEY'RE NOT MAKING IT EASY TO SAY GOOD-BYE.

SO MUCH OF MY ADULT LIFE IS TIED UP HERE. EVEN THESE *HALLS* SEEM LIKE OLD FRIENDS.

WHAT WAS IT MA USED TO SAY? "NEVER LOVE ANYTHING THAT CAN'T LOVE YOU BACK."

GOOD ADVICE, BUT I COULDN'T FOLLOW IT ANY MORE THAN SHE COULD!

MYSTERIOUS SUPERMAN SAVES SPACE PLANE

I'VE LOST TRACK OF HOW MANY TIMES I CHANGED INTO SUPERMAN'S WORKING CLOTHES IN THIS STOREROOM. IT'S HARD *NOT* TO FEEL NOSTALGIC OVER--!

STORAGE

UHUH-HUH-HUH

EH? SOMEONE'S CRYING? SUCH A FAINT, PLAINTIVE SOUND. IT'S COMING--

--FROM INSIDE THE STOREROOM!

ALICE?

ALICE? ARE YOU ALL RIGHT IN THERE?

NOK NOK

STORAG

OH, NO! SOMEBODY HEARD?!

WH--WHO'S THERE?

IT'S CLARK KENT, ALICE. LOIS TOLD ME THE PARTY WAS YOUR IDEA... I WANTED TO THANK YOU.

NO... NO... NO... NO...

ALICE?

NO! DON'T COME IN!

I THOUGHT I HEARD YOU CRYING. ARE YOU--?

I'M OKAY-- REALLY!

I'M SORRY, I DON'T MEAN TO PRY, BUT... ARE YOU ILL? THAT SLEEPING BAG--!

NO, I... I... OH, WHAT'S THE USE?

I LIVE HERE.

GREAT CAESAR'S GHOST, YOU'VE BEEN LIVING AT THE PLANET?!

ALICE... WHY?

WHITE

I HAD NOWHERE ELSE TO GO.

EXTECH

I—I'D LIVED IN THE SAME APARTMENT ALL MY LIFE...WITH MAMA.

"MAMA HAD ALWAYS READ THE PLANET, AND SHE WAS SO VERY PROUD WHEN I GOT INTO THE PAPER'S HIGH SCHOOL INTERNSHIP PROGRAM. I'D PLANNED TO BRING HER UP HERE, TO MEET ALL OF YOU...

"...BUT I NEVER GOT THE CHANCE.

MED ONE LEXCORP

"YOU HAVE TO UNDERSTAND,...MAMA WAS IN HER FORTIES WHEN I WAS BORN. SHE WAS ALWAYS FRAIL, AND AFTER PAPA DIED,...WELL, SHE NEVER REALLY GOT OVER LOSING HIM.

MERRY CHRISTMAS

GET WELL SOON.

HAPPY HOL

"SHE WAS IN THE HOSPITAL FOR NEARLY THREE MONTHS. SHE HELD ON FOR ONE LAST CHRISTMAS WITH ME.

"HER FINAL ILLNESS WIPED OUT OUR SAVINGS, AND THEN SOME. STILL, BY THEN, I WAS WORKING HERE FULL-TIME... I MIGHT HAVE MANAGED TO KEEP THE APARTMENT—

FINAL NOTICE

"--IF THE LANDLORD HADN'T DECIDED TO CONVERT THE PLACE TO CONDOS. WHEN I COULDN'T RAISE THE DOWN PAYMENT, HE HAD ME EVICTED."

I GOT A ROOM AT THE YWCA, AND TRIED TO FIND ANOTHER PLACE, BUT RENTS IN METROPOLIS ARE SO HIGH...

...AND THE RENTAL AGENTS ALL WANTED THREE MONTHS' SECURITY DEPOSIT, PLUS THE FIRST MONTH'S RENT IN ADVANCE! I COULDN'T AFFORD THAT!

I CHECKED SOME OUT-OF-TOWN LISTINGS, BUT I COULDN'T AFFORD THE RENT AND THE COST OF COMMUTING!

I COULDN'T STAY AT THE "Y" FOREVER, AND I WAS SCARED TO DEATH OF THE SHELTERS. I NEEDED SOMETHING I COULD HOLD ONTO. THE PLANET WAS THE ONLY LIFE I HAD LEFT! S-S-SO.... I JUST...MOVED IN.

SHHH... EASY, EASY! IT'S OKAY!

THAT WAS... TH-THREE Y-YEARS AGO!

BUT HOW DID YOU LIVE HERE ALL THAT TIME WITHOUT BEING NOTICED?

I WAS THE ALL-PURPOSE INTERN.... I HAD KEYS TO MOST OFFICES...

...I COOKED IN THE KITCHENETTE, SHOWERED IN THE COMPANY HEALTH CLUB, SLEPT IN THE STOREROOMS. MOSTLY, THOUGH, I WORKED ...NIGHT SHIFT AS WELL AS DAYS. IT KEPT MY MIND OFF ...THINGS.

I KEPT TRYING TO SAVE MONEY FOR AN APARTMENT... BUT THE RENTS KEPT GOING UP, TOO. BESIDES, I'M STILL PAYING OFF MAMA'S MEDICAL BILLS.

YOU WERE ALWAYS HERE, NO MATTER HOW EARLY I CAME IN. I USED TO KID YOU ABOUT IT... ASKING IF YOU LIVED HERE.

YOU SMILED AND TOLD ME YOU HAD A COT IN A STOREROOM... AND I THOUGHT YOU WERE JOKING!

I HAD TO JOKE ABOUT IT... I COULDN'T LET YOU KNOW I WAS REALLY LIVING HERE. I...

...I WAS TOO ASHAMED.

ALICE, YOU HAVE NOTHING TO BE ASHAMED OF... YOU DID NOTHING WRONG! WHAT HAPPENED TO YOU HAPPENS TO A LOT OF PEOPLE...

...I KNOW! I'VE SEEN ARMY WIDOWS STRUGGLE TO GET BY ON THEIR HUSBAND'S DEATH BENEFITS.

YEAH, AFTER MY DAD WAS REPORTED MISSING IN ACTION, MY MOM ALMOST LOST EVERYTHING! IF MY GRANDPARENTS HADN'T BEEN THERE TO HELP, I DON'T KNOW WHAT WE'D HAVE DONE!

LOIS AND JIM ARE RIGHT, ALICE. A LOT OF PEOPLE LIVE CLOSE TO THE EDGE. MY PARENTS STILL FARM A SMALL PIECE OF LAND IN KANSAS--

--AND IT SEEMS LIKE EVERY YEAR THEY FACE A DROUGHT OR A DELUGE... OR BOTH! I HELP THEM AS MUCH AS I CAN.

I'D HAVE OFFERED TO HELP YOU, TOO, IF I'D KNOWN.

WE ALL WOULD HAVE HELPED!

THAT'S VERY NICE OF YOU, BUT...

NO, ALICE--NO "BUTS"! YOU'VE BEEN STRUGGLING ALONE FOR TOO LONG. I WON'T ALLOW YOU TO SPEND ANOTHER CHRISTMAS IN SOME... STOREROOM!

IN FACT, IT'S TIME WE REMINDED THE WHOLE CITY WHAT THIS SEASON IS ABOUT!

CHIEF, WHAT--?

HELLO, MANNY? YEAH, AND A HAPPY CHANUKAH TO YOU! HAS PAGE ONE BEEN SET UP YET? GOOD! NO, HOLD OFF ON IT...

"...THERE'S SOMETHING I WANT TO ADD!"

DAILY PLANET

ARMS TREATY SIGNED AT LAST

THE GIVING SEASON
Editorial by Perry White

140

For a few weeks every December, we all seem to go a little crazy. Or perhaps it's the rest of the year when we're crazy, and this is the season when we regain our sanity.

Whatever the case, we act as if we've suddenly found something good in all of us. We want to laugh and sing and celebrate our wonderful discovery.

Then, come the first of the year, the celebrations abruptly end and we go back to grousing about our jobs and our taxes and what a rotten deal we've got.

But it doesn't have to be that way. With a little effort, we can hang onto this feeling of good will. With a little thought, we might realize how lucky most of us are.

Look around, and you'll see that some of us are not so well off. Some have no jobs to grouse about. Some do not have enough to eat.

Others sleep huddled in doorways or over gratings, using copies of this paper to keep warm.

These unfortunates are our brothers and sisters. But all too often we look away as they pass.

It's about time we stopped doing that.

It's about time we reminded ourselves that the shabbily dressed stranger shuffling by is another human being.

Maybe he's not a "worthless bum"...maybe he's just had a run of bad luck.

But we'll never know unless we make an effort to find out.

Every day, our newspapers and television bring us news of suffering around the world, and it often seems too much to take.

Perhaps that is why we try to ignore the misery closer to home. Perhaps we look away out of guilt or embarrassment or anger. And perhaps some of us look away out of fear --

-- that little more than a single paycheck keeps us from joining the ranks of the homeless.

But whatever our reasons, we cannot continue this way. Precious lives are being wasted, and it diminishes us all to allow such a thing. This is our problem, and we must not run away from it.

A frightening, growing percentage of our city's homeless are families, often single-parent families.

Imagine what it's like to be that child.

Imagine what it's like to have no home for your child at Christmas.

What hope is there for these new homeless?

By, now, a lot of you are probably throwing up your hands in despair. "I'm not Superman!" you cry, "What can I do??"

The answer is simply: whatever you can!

142

No one is asking you to save the world, and it's not necessary that you be able to fly.

People like yourselves are already working with a score of organizations -- from the Metropolis Human Services Coalition to the Salvation Army.

These organizations do as good a job as they can, but they could do better with your help.

WELCOME TO ALL!

The kitchens and the missions work with the most needy, providing food, shelter, and warm clothing.

Your donations of clothing can give Christmas to those who would have missed it.

Your donations of food can help give homeless people the strength to go on another day.

143

And your donations of time will keep these organizations running, as will your donations of money. Whatever you can give, whatever you can do, will help.

But, please, don't think you can just write a check and forget about the homeless for another year.

This is a problem that will not be solved overnight...not even with Superman's help.

Some of our city's homeless are tormented by mental problems...

...it will take an extra effort to win their trust.

Others cannot turn their backs on drugs or alcohol...

...For them, we may be able to offer little more than our prayers.

Metropolis is a prosperous city, but with each passing year good, hard-working men and women find it more difficult to find affordable housing here.

Every year, there are more luxury condos and fewer row homes. This, too, is part of the problem we must not forget when January arrives.

There are many ways we can attack the problem. We can petition our city council to create incentives for the construction of more low- and middle-income housing.

We can donate time and labor to organizations such as Habitat for Humanity or the Bakerline Neighborhood Housing Service. But we must do something...

ALICE? ARE YOU ALL RIGHT?

OH.... YES, I'M FINE. I GUESS I JUST GET A LITTLE MELANCHOLY AROUND CHRISTMAS. THIS WAS MAMA'S FAVORITE TIME OF YEAR.

I UNDERSTAND.

THIS IS SO NICE OF YOU, MRS. WHITE ...LETTING ME IMPOSE ON YOUR HOLIDAY... AND ON SUCH SHORT NOTICE.

IT'S NO IMPOSITION. AND, PLEASE, CALL ME.... ALICE.

OH, DEAR.... THAT MAY CAUSE SOME CONFUSION.

MAMA ALWAYS CALLED ME ALLIE...

ALLIE IT IS, THEN!

I'VE BEEN DOING SOME FIGURING, AND THE WAY I SEE IT, YOU'VE BEEN PUTTING IN AT LEAST A HALF-SHIFT IN OVERTIME FOR THREE YEARS, WITHOUT PROPER COMPENSATION. I'D SAY THE PLANET OWES YOU PLENTY.

BUT I DIDN'T--!

LET ME FINISH! I'M GOING TO USE THAT FACT AS A WEDGE TO PRY A LIVING WAGE OUT OF MANAGEMENT FOR YOU -- SO THAT YOU CAN AFFORD A DECENT PLACE OF YOUR OWN.

UNTIL YOU DO, YOU CAN STAY HERE!

HERE? WITH YOU AND MRS. WHITE?

OF COURSE, ALLIE. EVER SINCE OUR SON JERRY MOVED OUT, WE'VE HAD MORE ROOM THAN WE NEED! YOU'RE MORE THAN WELCOME TO STAY.

OH, THANK YOU.... THANK YOU!

UH-HMPH... YOU'RE WELCOME, OF COURSE...

....DON'T MENTION IT... REALLY.

LATER, A FEW MILES OUTSIDE OF SMALLVILLE, KANSAS...

OH, MY! YES...

...I DO BELIEVE THAT THIS IS GOING TO BE ONE OF MY BEST MINCE PIES EVER!

I'D SAY YOU'RE RIGHT!

IT SMELLS SO GOOD, I HOMED IN ON THE AROMA! IN FACT, I THINK THE 81ST AIRBORNE IS RIGHT BEHIND ME!

MERRY CHRISTMAS, MA! SORRY I'M SO LATE.

OH, THAT'S ALL RIGHT, DEAR. WE JUST GOT BACK FROM THE CANDLELIGHT SERVICE AT CHURCH OURSELVES.

ON INTO THE LIVING ROOM WITH YOU NOW! PA HAS A SURPRISE FOR YOU!

MERRY CHRISTMAS, PA! MA SAID... LANA!

AW, YOU FIGURED OUT MY SURPRISE! HEH-HEH!

MERRY CHRISTMAS, CLARK.

I DIDN'T KNOW YOU WERE OUT OF THE HOSPITAL!

THEY RELEASED ME JUST THIS AFTERNOON. YOUR FOLKS PICKED ME UP.

DIDN'T SEEM RIGHT FOR HER TO BE ALONE AT CHRISTMAS.

BUSY NIGHT, SON?

VERY BUSY, PA. AND YOU'RE RIGHT... NO ONE SHOULD HAVE TO BE ALONE ... ESPECIALLY AT THIS TIME OF YEAR. I'M GLAD YOU'RE HERE, LANA. IT'S GOOD TO SEE YOU UP AND AROUND.

IT'S GOOD TO BE UP AND AROUND AND TO BE HERE WITH ALL OF YOU.

I SPENT SEVERAL CHRISTMASES ALONE AFTER AUNT HELEN PASSED ON... THEY WEREN'T MUCH FUN.

TOO MANY PEOPLE *NEVER KNOW* THE JOY OF THIS SEASON. FOR SOME, IT'S ALL THEY CAN DO TO FIND FOOD AND SHELTER. YOU TRY TO MAKE THINGS BETTER, BUT IT'S A NEVER-ENDING STRUGGLE.

IT'S NOT YOUR STRUGGLE *ALONE*, SON. IF THERE'S ANY PURPOSE IN THIS LIFE, IT'S TO HELP OTHERS ALONG!

AMEN TO *THAT!* WE'RE JUST HAPPY THAT YOU CAN TAKE TIME TO BE WITH US, CLARK.

I AM SO *BLESSED*... WE ALL ARE.

EGG NOG, ANYONE?

MMMM... SOUNDS GOOD TO ME!

A *TOAST*--HERE'S TO FAMILY AND GOOD FRIENDS! MAY WE ALL FIND THE FORTITUDE TO KEEP THE SPIRIT OF SHARING ALIVE ALL THE YEAR!

Seasons Greetings

HAPPY HOLIDAYS

AND MAY WE ALL COME TOGETHER, HEALTHY AND HAPPY, FOR MANY CHRISTMASES TO COME!

HEAR, HEAR.

MERRY CHRISTMAS, ONE AND ALL!

YES... ONE AND ALL!

May the blessings of the season be with you and yours! Rog, Dan, Art, Al, Glenn, Jon & Mike

THE TENSION FILLED NASA TRACKING CENTER IN HOUSTON.

ANY SIGN OF TEAM EXCALIBUR YET?

NOTHING. NADA. ZIP.

THAT EXPLOSION ON BOARD MAY HAVE FORCED THEM INTO A CONDITION RED RE-ENTRY, BUT LET'S FACE IT--

C'MON, GARRISON, PULL THAT NOSE UP!

WHATCHA THINK I'M TRYIN' TA DO?

"--THEIR INCOMING TRAJECTORY WAS FAR TOO SHARP! CHANCES ARE THE EXCALIBUR HAS BURNED UP BY NOW!"

WELL, TRY HARDER! IF YOU DON'T--

WHAT STEVEN IS TRYING TO EXPLAIN, JIM, IS THAT ONE WAY OR ANOTHER WE'RE COUNTING ON YOU TO--

SHADDUP WILLYA?! THIS WEIRD RADIATION'S EATIN' AWAY AT EVERY CONTROL--

--AND THE SHIP IS SHAKIN' MORE THAN A HULA DANCER ON A BUCKIN' BRONCO! SO LEAVE ME ALONE--

--AND CLIMB INTO THOSE SURVIVAL SUITS WHILE YOU GOT THE CHANCE!

SUPERMAN® The LIMITS of POWER

Created by
JERRY SIEGEL &
JOE SHUSTER

DAN JURGENS
STORY AND LAYOUTS

FINISHES: "DICK" GIORDANO
LETTERER: ALBERT DE GUZMAN
COLORIST: GLENN WHITMORE
LT. HONCHO: JON PETERSON
HONCHO: MIKE CARLIN

2

T-TERRI?

TERRI?

O-OVER HERE-- HANK...

DARLING! PLEASE, TELL ME YOU'RE ALL RIGHT!

I-I THINK SO... BUT YOUR HAIR! IT'S TURNED COMPLETELY WHITE! WHAT'S GOING ON HERE?

I WOULD IMAGINE THE RADIATION CAUSED IT WHEN IT BROKE CONTAINMENT.

HAVE YOU SEEN ANYTHING OF JIM OR STEVEN?

HELP!

HELP ME!

IT CAN'T BE--

--BUT THAT'S STEVEN'S VOICE!

SORT OF.

3

HANK, WHAT IS IT? WHAT'S HAPPENED TO STEVEN?

A PHENOMENON SO WILD AND STARTLING I'D NOT THOUGHT IT POSSIBLE!

THOSE RADIATION EXPERIMENTS WE WERE PERFORMING ON BOARD HAVE SOMEHOW MUTATED HIM!

FEEL SO-- LIKE I'M NOT EVEN HERE...

I CAN ONLY SPECULATE AT THIS POINT, BUT IT'S ENTIRELY POSSIBLE YOU ARE NOW WITHOUT MASS.

THE RADIATION MUST HAVE RIFLED THROUGH YOUR BODY WHEN IT WAS DESTROYED IN THE CRASH! YET MIRACULOUSLY YOUR MIND SURVIVED--

--AND SOMEHOW FORMED THAT RADIATION INTO A NEW BODY!

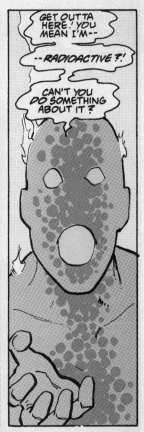

GET OUTTA HERE! YOU MEAN I'M--

--RADIOACTIVE?!

CAN'T YOU DO SOMETHING ABOUT IT?

HMM... IF I HAD ACCESS TO NASA'S LABS--

OH, MAN! AM I GONNA BE OKAY? AM I GONNA DIE?

WAIT A MINUTE! WHERE'S JIM?

FAN OUT-- WE MUST FIND HIM QUICKLY!

OH... GOD... NO...

AWWW... NOT HIM TOO!

OH--

--JIM?

TEAM EXCALIBUR

4

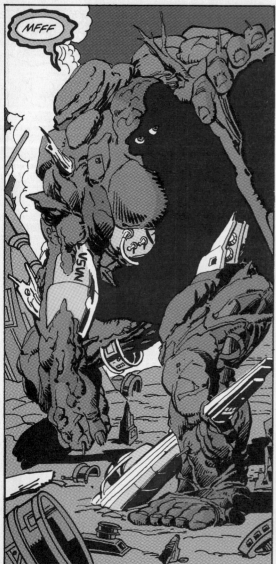

MFFF

BY THE STARS, MAN-- --WHAT'S HAPPENED TO YOU?

TELL ME THAT'S NOT YOU, JIM.... SAY SOMETHING.... ANYTH--

NNNGH

NO....! JIM.... ARE YOU--

HANK, LOOK AT HIM.... HE'S OBVIOUSLY IN PAIN! BUT WE CAN'T POSSIBLY HELP HIM --

--WHEN WE CAN'T EXPLAIN HOW WE EVEN SURVIVED!

INDEED. BOTH JIM AND STEVE SHOULD HAVE EXPIRED IN THAT CRASH.

HOWEVER, JUST AS STEVEN SOMEHOW REASSEMBLED A BODY OUT OF RADIATION--

--JIM'S MIND USED ROCK, GRAVEL, BRANCHES AND THE WRECKAGE OF THE SHUTTLE TO DO THE SAME.

SEEMINGLY AN IMPOSSIBLE FEAT, YET THE EVIDENCE IS CLEAR.

5

THIS IS ALL THEORY, OF COURSE, BUT REMEMBER THAT WE *WERE* EXPERIMENTING WITH THAT RADIATION WHEN WE RAN INTO TROUBLE.

AND IT HAD FANTASTIC PROPERTIES WHICH DEVIATED FROM ANYTHING WE'D SEEN BEFORE. ADD THE SOLAR FLARES--

AND WE WERE ALL AFFECTED SOMEHOW! WHAT NOW?

PROPRIETY DEMANDS RETURNING TO NASA--

--BUT WE HAVEN'T THE TIME! CONSIDERING IT WAS A *LEXCORP* BUILT EXPERIMENT, I SAY WE HEAD TO METROPOLIS.

NOW THAT I THINK ABOUT IT, THE LEXCORP EQUIPMENT TROUBLED ME FROM THE START!

HEY, GANG, CATCH THIS!

NOT ONLY CAN I FLY, BUT I CAN CREATE A *PLATFORM* FOR YOU TO RIDE ON!

OF COURSE, SINCE YOU LACK A CONVENTIONAL PHYSICAL PRESENCE, YOUR NEW ABILITIES SHOULD BE LIMITLESS.

HONEY, ARE YOU SURE WE'RE DOING THE RIGHT THING?

UNDOUBTEDLY. JIM'S AGONY IS SO SEVERE I DOUBT HE CAN SURVIVE LONG.

NOT TO MENTION THE RADIATION SICKNESS I CAN FEEL EATING ITS WAY INTO ME. BUT I CAN'T LET THEM KNOW--

--JUST HOW SLIM OUR CHANCES MIGHT BE.

ALL RIGHT, STEVEN, NEXT STOP--

NASA

United

"--METROPOLIS!"

--CLARK KENT!

YOU KNOW, LITTLE SISTER, I ALWAYS THOUGHT FLIGHT ATTENDANTS WERE SUPPOSED TO BE POLITE AND TACTFUL!

WE'RE NOT ON A 747, LOIS!

BINGO! AND THIS DINNER IS JUST FOR TWO!

SO, UNLESS YOU PLAN TO SERVE IT TO US--

BING BONG

HEY, YOU KNOW I GOT NOTHING AGAINST THE GUY, LOIS!

IT REALLY JUST BOWLS ME OVER TO THINK YOU'RE COOKING THIS FIVE-STAR DINNER FOR--

HI, LUCY! I DIDN'T KNOW YOU WERE JOINING US TONIGHT!

LOOOIS, MR. RIGHT IS HERE!

LUCY!

OOOPS! SOUNDS LIKE MY CUE TO GO! SEE YOU, KIDS!

HMM... SEEING CLARK REMINDS ME OF SOMEONE I HAVEN'T SEEN IN A LONG TIME!

JIMMY OLSEN AND I HAD SOME PRETTY GOOD TIMES TOGETHER! MAYBE IT'S TIME I LOOK HIM UP!

IT'S REALLY NICE OF YOU TO HAVE ME OVER, LOIS. DESPITE MA'S EFFORTS AT TEACHING ME--

-- I'M NOT MUCH OF A COOK. AS FOR OUR... RELATIONSHIP...

UGH-- I HATE THAT WORD! LET'S JUST KEEP THINGS LIGHT AND SEE WHERE THE TIDE TAKES US, OKAY?

BING BONG

LOOKS LIKE LUCY FORGOT HER KEYS AGAIN!

OH!

IT'S YOU!

7

SORRY TO INTERRUPT, BUT I KNEW YOU WANTED TO STUDY THESE PAPERS BEFORE MONDAY, LOIS!

GLAD TO, PERRY, STARTING *TOMORROW*.

HI, PERRY. YOU AND ALICE ARE LOOKING GOOD AS EVER!

WE'LL GET OUT OF YOUR WAY, NOW, LOIS!

GOODBYE, MR. KENT.

UHH... NICE SEEING YOU, ALICE, IT'S BEEN A WHILE.

YOU SHOULD HAVE EXPECTED THAT WHEN YOU STABBED MY HUSBAND IN THE *BACK*, MR. KENT!

HUH?

YOU HEARD ME, MR. NEWSTIME!

PERRY TOOK YOUR ROOKIE MIND OFF THE STREETS AND MOLDED IT INTO A WRITER'S!

B-B-BUT--

SO HOW DO YOU PAY HIM BACK? YOU NOT ONLY QUIT, BUT YOU HAVE THE GALL TO COME CRAWLING BACK *BEGGING* FOR MERCY!

"YOU, MR. KENT, ARE A REAL STINKER!'"

THIS IS *RIDICULOUS!* MEETING RIGHT OUT HERE IN THE OPEN LIKE THIS!

IF ANYONE SPOTS ME--MORGAN EDGE, *ALLEGED CRIMINAL* --TALKING TO YOU-- MANNHEIM, *RUMORED* HEAD OF INTERGANG--

--THEY'LL PUT THE TWO OF US BEHIND BARS UNTIL THE NEXT *ICE AGE!*

INTERGANG WAS DOING FINE BEFORE WE HOOKED UP WITH YOU, EDGE... AND WE'LL BE FINE EVEN IF THEY NAIL *YOU* TO THE WALL!

THAT REMAINS TO BE SEEN. THE PROSE- CUTION HASN'T PROVEN *ANYTHING* YET.

AND, AGAINST OUR BETTER JUDGMENT, WE'VE TAKEN STEPS TO KEEP IT THAT WAY!

SO JUST PLAY DUMB AND YOU'LL COME OUT OF THIS SMELLIN' LIKE A ROSE.

LISTEN UGLY... I DON'T NEED YOUR HELP!

THE NAME'S MANNHEIM-- AND I'M ON *YOUR* SIDE!

DON'T FORGET THAT-- --AND WE WON'T!

I DON'T WANT ANYONE *HIT*-- I CAN'T AFFORD IT!

YOU *HAD* AN EQUAL SAY AT ONE POINT-- NOW *WE'RE* CALLIN' THE SHOTS!

SO IF I WAS YOU, I'D STEER CLEAR OF CAT GRANT AND *ALL* HER FRIENDS--

--DO THAT, AND YOU'LL GET OFF *SCOT FREE!*

NO WITNESSES... NO TESTIMONIES... NO *CONVICTIONS!*

HERE WE ARE, GANG! LEXCORP, METROPOLIS!

I JUST PRAY WE STILL HAVE TIME! EVEN HANK IS LOOKING SICK NOW!

INDEED. THAT RADIATION IS FINALLY STARTING TO TAKE ITS TOLL ON ME.

I WONDER-- WILL ITS EFFECTS BE SIMILAR TO JIM'S AND STEVE'S--

--OR WILL IT BE SOMETHING ALTOGETHER DIFFERENT?

NO MATTER. WE CAN ONLY CONCERN OURSELVES WITH THE PRESENT.

HEY, I DON'T KNOW WHAT YOU FREAKOS ARE DOIN' HERE, BUT IF YOU'RE SMART YOU'LL FREEZE BEFORE I BLAST YA!

9

THIS HERE IS LEXCORP PRIVATE PROPERTY AND WE GOT STRICT ORDERS TO BURN VIOLATORS!

AW, KNOCK OFF THE DEPUTY ACT, BARNEY!

IT IS ABSOLUTELY IMPERATIVE THAT WE GAIN ACCESS TO THIS COMPLEX'S RADIATION LABORATORY--

--AND PERHAPS CONSULT WITH LEX LUTHOR HIMSELF!

YOU GOTTA BETTER CHANCE OF SEEIN' ELVIS AT GRACELAND! NOW, TAKE MAN-MOUNTAIN-MIKE HERE AND BEAT IT!

LIVES ARE AT STAKE HERE, MAN! DON'T FORCE US TO HAVE TO BREAK IN!

LEXCORP SECURITY CENTER TO SENTRY TWO!

MOVE AWAY FROM THOSE FOLKS FAST! SENSORS SHOW THEY'RE CONTAMINATED WITH RADIATION THAT GOES OFF THE SCALE!

R--R--RADIATION?

LISSEN, CALL UP THOSE GUYS IN THE G-LEVEL WARSUITS PRONTO...

"...'CUZ I'M OUTTA HERE!"

TELEPHONE CALL FOR YOU, PERRY. IT'S THE CITY DESK.

OKAY, LESTER, SHOOT.

FOUR RADIOACTIVE PARANORMALS ARE INVADING LEXCORP?! WOW!

SEND THE BEST PHOTOGRAPHER YOU CAN FIND! I'M ON MY WAY!

C'MON, LOIS! LET'S HIT THE STREETS!

LOOK, CLARK, SOMEONE HAS TO STAY AND WATCH DINNER AND SINCE YOU'RE JUST A FREELANCER--

--PUH-LEASE BE A DEAR AND DO THAT? CIAO!

SURE, LOIS, WHATEVER YOU WANT.

10

RIGHT.

WAS IT BECAUSE I'M NO LONGER ON STAFF?

KIND OF SURPRISED THAT PERRY DIDN'T ASK ME TO JOIN THEM.

OR DOES HE FEEL THE SAME ABOUT ME AS HIS WIFE DOES?

GUESS I WOULDN'T BLAME HIM IF HE DID.

THOSE THINGS SHE SAID REALLY STRUCK HOME-- AND I HAD IT COMING!

I TREATED PERRY PRETTY BAD --MORE THAN I'D--HEY!

THERE REALLY ARE SOME PARANORMALS TRYING TO BREAK INTO LEXCORP!

BETTER BE CAREFUL HERE--IF THESE GUYS HAVE A GRUDGE AGAINST LUTHOR IT'S QUITE POSSIBLE THEY MIGHT BE JUSTIFIED IN THEIR ACTIONS!

NOW, EVERYBODY COOL IT UNTIL I FIGURE OUT WHAT THE HECK'S GOING ON HERE!

SUPERMAN?!

NO--LOOKS LIKE LUTHOR'S GOON IS GONNA BLAST HIM WITH THAT WRIST GAUNTLET!

DON'T KNOW IF SUPERMAN IS TOUGH ENOUGH TO TAKE IT--

--WHICH MEANS I GOTTA NAIL THAT CLOWN FIRST!

BLAST! SUPERMAN MOVED RIGHT IN MY LINE OF FIRE! HE'S GONNA BE TICKED OFF NOW!

HEY!

UH-OH...

LOOK, HANK! SUPERMAN'S ARRIVED!

IF WE CAN JUST GET HIM TO HELP US WE MIGHT IMPROVE OUR ODDS!

INDEED! BUT WILL HE LISTEN TO FOUR APPARENT LAW BREAKERS?

OH, NO! GARRISON'S INADVERTENTLY HURLED THE GUARD RIGHT AT THE MAN OF STEEL! WE'RE DOOMED!

BIZARRE-- BOTH SIDES ARE OUT TO ATTACK ME--

--AND A COUPLE OF THESE PEOPLE ARE EVEN WEARING NASA SURVIVAL SUITS!

BKAMMM

12

159

SUPERMAN'S SCREWED EVERYTHING UP! WE'RE NEVER GONNA GET INSIDE AND GET CURED--

--UNLESS I GET HIM AND ALL THESE GUARDS OUTTA HERE!

I'VE HAD IT WITH ALL OF YOU! CAN'T YOU JUST LEAVE US ALONE?

CAN'T YOU GET OFF OUR BACKS?

THE PRESSURE AND RADIATION HAVE FINALLY GOTTEN TO STEVEN!

HE'S DISTRAUGHT-- ALMOST COMPLETELY BERSERK!

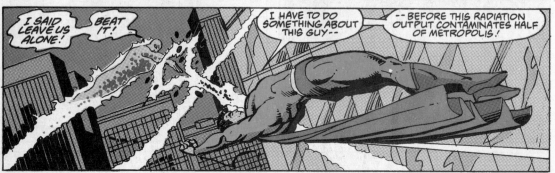

I SAID LEAVE US ALONE!

BEAT IT!

I HAVE TO DO SOMETHING ABOUT THIS GUY--

-- BEFORE THIS RADIATION OUTPUT CONTAMINATES HALF OF METROPOLIS!

IF I CAN'T GET RID OF HIM I'LL HAVE TO CONTAIN HIM SOMEHOW--

-- AND THESE UPGRADED BATTLE SUITS OF LUTHOR'S SHOULD DO THE TRICK!

GO! GO AWAY!

THESE ARE BUILT TO WITHSTAND MORE THAN THEIR PREDECESSORS!

ONCE I MELT IT ALL TOGETHER WITH HEAT VISION--

NO! NO!

-- I SHOULD HAVE A NIFTY COCOON TO WRAP THIS GUY IN!

13

160

KRAK

¡UGH!¿

B KOO M

LEXCORP

QUITE A RAP! WHO ARE THESE GUYS, ANYWAY?

AND WHERE DID THEY COME INTO CONTACT WITH ENOUGH RADIATION TO MUTATE THEM THIS WAY?

WAIT, SUPERMAN, BEFORE ACTING AGAINST US YOU MUST HEAR US OUT!

I'M HANK HENSHAW AND WE JUST RETURNED FROM A TOP SECRET DEFENSE MISSION IN SPACE.

ONE OF OUR TASKS WAS TO TEST SOME NEW RADIATION EQUIPMENT THAT REQUIRED ZERO GRAVITY... FOR LEXCORP!

THAT EXPLAINS YOUR PRESENCE HERE, I GUESS.

IN FACT, I WOULDN'T PUT IT PAST LUTHOR TO BE UP TO SOMETHING FISHY.

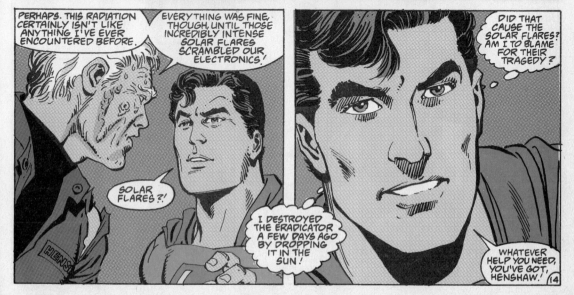

PERHAPS. THIS RADIATION CERTAINLY ISN'T LIKE ANYTHING I'VE EVER ENCOUNTERED BEFORE.

EVERYTHING WAS FINE, THOUGH, UNTIL THOSE INCREDIBLY INTENSE SOLAR FLARES SCRAMBLED OUR ELECTRONICS!

SOLAR FLARES?!

I DESTROYED THE ERADICATOR A FEW DAYS AGO BY DROPPING IT IN THE SUN!

DID THAT CAUSE THE SOLAR FLARES? AM I TO BLAME FOR THEIR TRAGEDY?

WHATEVER HELP YOU NEED, YOU'VE GOT, HENSHAW!

14

WHAT A *SURPRISE!* WHEN I HEARD THE DOORBELL RING--

--I NEVER EXPECTED YOU TO BE THE GUY PUSHING THE BUTTON!

IT'S BEEN A LONG TIME, GOOD LOOKING.

SO, WHAT BRINGS THE ILLUSTRIOUS JOSE DELGADO TO MY NECK OF THE WOODS?

ILLUSTRIOUS? THAT'S A LAUGH!

ACTUALLY, I WAS JUST ON MY WAY OVER TO TELL LOIS I'D BE BUNKING AT THE "Y" FOR A WHILE--

--AND I DECIDED TO STOP IN AND SEE HOW YOU FELT ABOUT THE OTHER NEWS!

NEWS? WHAT NEWS?

I THOUGHT YOU *KNEW!*

LOOK, YOUR EX-HUSBAND HAS HIRED ME--AS *GANGBUSTER*--TO BE YOUR BODYGUARD DURING THE EDGE TRIAL!

HE'S WORRIED THAT *INTERGANG* MIGHT COME AFTER YOU!

BODYGUARD?! NO OFFENSE, JOSE--

--BUT THE LAST THING I NEED IS SOMEONE MAKING LIKE MY SHADOW!

LISTEN, LADY YOU'RE IN DANGER HERE--

--AND SO IS YOUR KID! BESIDES... I'VE ALREADY SPENT THE ADVANCE.

SO JUST AS SOON AS I'M DONE AT LOIS'S--

--GANGBUSTER IS GONNA BE STICKING TO YOU LIKE GLUE!

15

BLAST IT ALL!

THE RADIATION IS AFFECTING ALL OF US NOW! TERRI'S FADING FROM OUR PLANE OF REALITY-- GARRISON'S IN AGONY--

--AND I AM TOTALLY UNABLE TO HELP THEM!

HENSHAW, YOU'RE EXHAUSTED-- YOU'VE GOTTA GET SOME REST!

REST?! LOOK AT ME? IF I SLEEP NOW I MAY NEVER WAKE UP!

WE'RE DYING, SUPERMAN--

--AND I CAN'T SAVE US!

HANK--

--MAYBE WE SHOULD TRY S.T.A.R. LABS!

LUTHOR'S NOT HERE TO HELP REVERSE THE PROCESS AND I'M NO SCIENTIST!

NO! ONLY MY BRILLIANCE IS EQUAL TO THIS CHALLENGE!

HE'S IRRATIONAL NOW... CAN'T SAY AS I BLAME HIM--OR ANY OF THEM.

IF ONLY I KNEW MORE ABOUT KRYPTON'S ADVANCED SCIENCES I MIGHT BE ABLE TO CURE THEM ....

H-HANK! WHAT'S GOING ON? I'M BECOMING A PHANTOM!

SCANNERS REVEAL THE RADIATION IS CAUSING YOU TO BLEED INTO ANOTHER DIMENSION!

OH, GOD...

FREE-- I'M FREE!

STEVE'S BURNED THROUGH THE COCOON-- AND HE'S HOTTER THAN EVER!

16

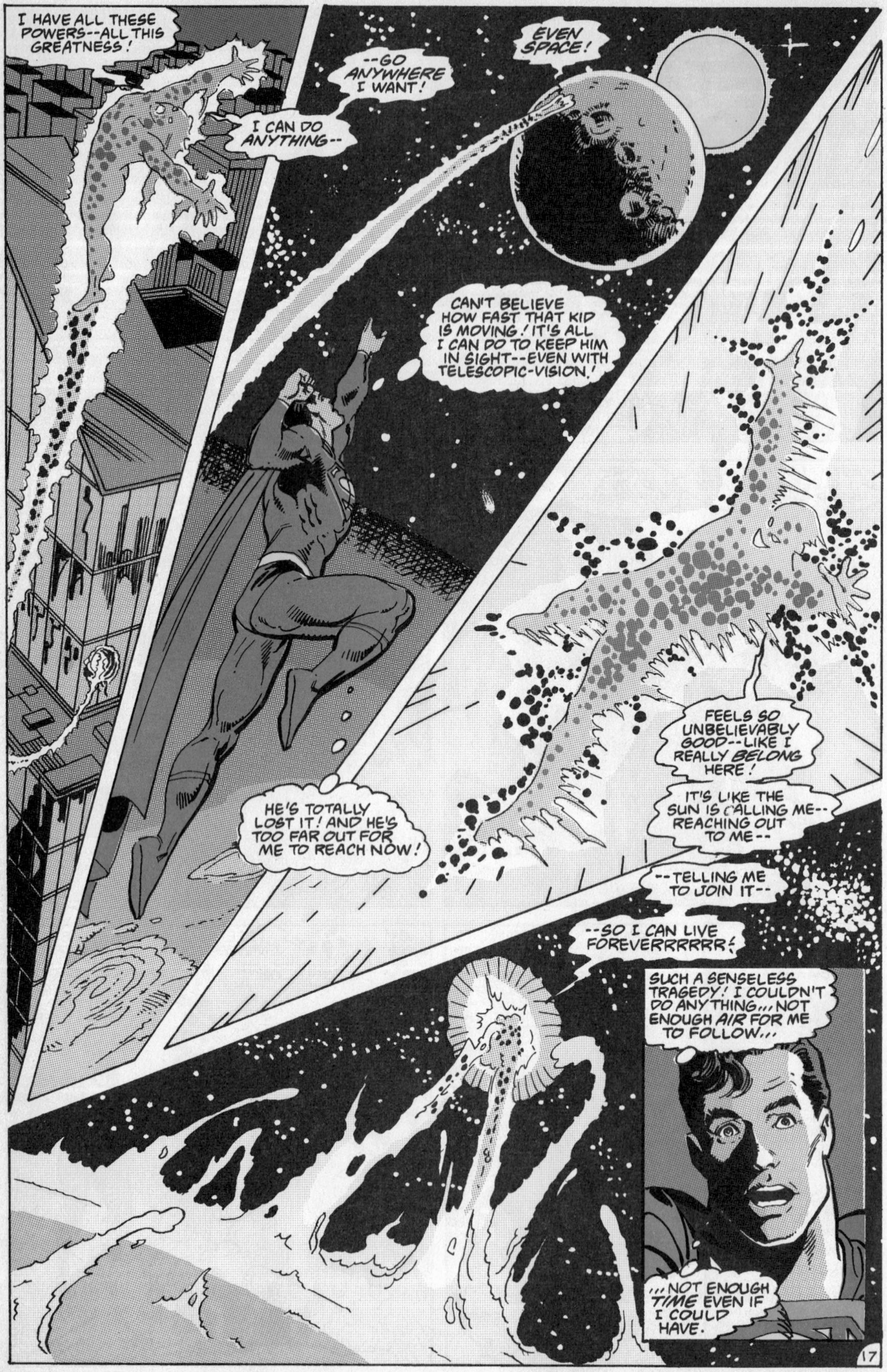
I HAVE ALL THESE POWERS--ALL THIS GREATNESS!
I CAN DO ANYTHING--
--GO ANYWHERE I WANT!
EVEN SPACE!
CAN'T BELIEVE HOW FAST THAT KID IS MOVING! IT'S ALL I CAN DO TO KEEP HIM IN SIGHT--EVEN WITH TELESCOPIC-VISION!
HE'S TOTALLY LOST IT! AND HE'S TOO FAR OUT FOR ME TO REACH NOW!
FEELS SO UNBELIEVABLY GOOD--LIKE I REALLY BELONG HERE!
IT'S LIKE THE SUN IS CALLING ME--REACHING OUT TO ME--
--TELLING ME TO JOIN IT--
--SO I CAN LIVE FOREVERRRRRR!
SUCH A SENSELESS TRAGEDY! I COULDN'T DO ANYTHING... NOT ENOUGH AIR FOR ME TO FOLLOW...
...NOT ENOUGH TIME EVEN IF I COULD HAVE.
17

I...UH....

THE OTHERS....!

HAVE TO GET BACK TO LEXCORP ...SEE IF I CAN'T AT LEAST SAVE THE OTHERS!

IF HANK HASN'T MADE A BREAKTHROUGH I'LL HAVE TO TRY SOMETHING ELSE....IT'S A LONG SHOT--

--BUT THE JLA OR TITANS MIGHT BE ABLE TO--!

NO! I'M TOO LATE!

HANK?

HANK?!

MMMPH?

NO...SUPERMAN, DEATH...HAS NOT YET CLAIMED... ME.

I AM... HOWEVER... BEYOND ;UHN; SAVING, AS IS... GARRISON.

MY WIFE... THOUGH... I ;UHN;--BEG YOU--

--SAVE HER BY USING--

--USING THE--

--UHFFFFF.

HANK! SAVE HER USING WHAT? WHAT?

HIS SUFFERING IS FINALLY ENDED!

MY DEAR HUSBAND....

TERRI-- I CAN HARDLY SEE YOU!

YES, THE VORTEX OF THE OTHER DIMENSION IS DRAWING ME IN!

18

MMMPH! NNNGG!

WAIT A MINUTE-- YOU KNOW WHAT HANK WAS TRYING TO DO, DON'T YOU?

MMMFF!

THROUGH THAT DOOR, EH?

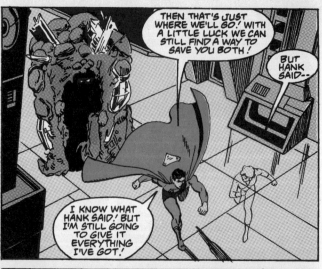

THEN THAT'S JUST WHERE WE'LL GO! WITH A LITTLE LUCK WE CAN STILL FIND A WAY TO SAVE YOU BOTH!

BUT HANK SAID--

I KNOW WHAT HANK SAID! BUT I'M STILL GOING TO GIVE IT EVERYTHING I'VE GOT!

THAT VAULT-- YOU THINK THAT'S WHAT HANK HAD IN MIND?

AS THICK AS THOSE CONCRETE WALLS ARE, I'D SAY IT'S SOME KIND OF RADIATION CHAMBER!

YOU MEAN HANK WAS PLANNING TO USE RADIATION ON US? HOW CAN THAT HELP?

MAYBE IT'S LIKE USING CHEMOTHERAPY ON A CANCER PATIENT...

IN ANY CASE, HANK PROGRAMMED THIS EQUIPMENT FROM THE COMPUTERS IN THE OTHER ROOM!

WE'VE GOT NOTHING TO LOSE BY TRYING!

NO KIDDING! I'M SO IMMATERIAL NOW--

--THAT I CAN EASILY PASS RIGHT THROUGH THIS WALL!

19

CAN'T HELP BUT SHAKE THE FEELING THAT THE *ERADICATOR* IS BEHIND ALL THIS...

BESIDES... CURING TERRI AND JIM IS THE PROBLEM AT HAND!

HANG ON IN THERE, KIDDO. WE'RE GOING FOR BROKE!

"AND WHEN WE'RE DONE WITH YOU IT'S GARRISON'S TURN!"

DANGER

Magnetic Resonance Imaging Booth

WARNING: Remove all metal objects from person before enter...

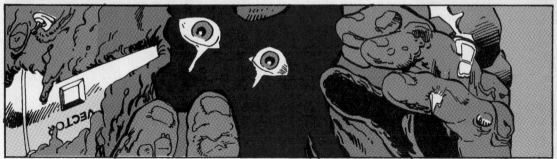

I'M GIVING YOU THE FULL DOSE OF RADIATION, TERRI! HOW YOU FEELING?

TERRI?

IT HURTS-- INCREDIBLY *PAINFUL!*

BUT IT'S *PHYSICAL* PAIN...

...IT MUST BE WORKING!

20

167

I'M ALIVE!

I'M WHOLE AGAIN!

WE'LL LET A DOCTOR DETERMINE THAT LATER! WE'VE GOT TO FIND GARRISON BEFORE IT'S TOO LATE!

I COULD'VE SWORN HE WAS RIGHT BEHIND US...

OF ALL OF US, HIS MANIFESTATION APPEARED TO BE THE MOST PAINFUL. I PRAY THAT WHEN WE FIND HIM WE'LL BE ABLE TO--

J-JIM?

OH.... NO....

WHY?

WHY DID HE DO IT?

HE--HE COMMITTED SUICIDE!

THAT MAGNETIC RESONANCE IMAGER CAN RIP A WATCH OFF A MAN FROM FIFTY FEET AWAY!

THE RADIATION --THE PAIN-- MUST'VE MADE HIM FEEL THAT THIS WAS HIS ONLY OPTION.

THEY'RE GONE-- ALL OF THEM!

WH- WHERE DO I GO FROM HERE?

WHEREVER YOU GO, I'LL DO MY BEST TO HELP!

IF I HADN'T CAUSED THIS BY THROWING THE ERADICATOR INTO THE SUN YESTERDAY AFTERNOON--

I DON'T KNOW WHAT ERADICATOR IS-- BUT IT COULDN'T HAVE CAUSED OUR MUTATION...

--THE SOLAR EXPLOSION RESPONSIBLE OCCURRED YESTERDAY MORNING!

IT'S SMALL CONSOLATION... CONSIDERING...

NO.... TEAM EXCALIBUR'S FATE WAS SIMPLY A TRAGIC ACCIDENT... AND NOTHING COULD HAVE SAVED US.

NOT EVEN A SUPERMAN, I GUESS.

C'MON, TERRI, YOU'RE IN SHOCK-- LET'S GET YOU TO A HOSPITAL.

21

THERE-- THAT SHOULD DO IT!

GOOD THING I TURNED OFF THE OVEN EARLIER OR THIS SOUFFLÉ WOULD BE A CINDER BY NOW.

A SLIGHT TOUCH OF HEAT VISION AND *VIOLA!* -- DONE TO A-- EH?

KEYS!

NO NEED FOR THOSE, LOIS. I'M STILL HERE!

GOSH, CLARK, I CAN'T BELIEVE YOU WAITED FOR ME!

SORRY IT TOOK SO LONG, BUT WHEN I TELL YOU ABOUT THE BLOCK-BUSTER HAPPENINGS AT LEXCORP--

WAIT.

I DON'T WANT TO TALK ABOUT LEXCORP, WORK OR ANYTHING ELSE....

...EXCEPT *US.*

MAYBE YOU WANT THIS RELATIONSHIP TO PROCEED AT ITS OWN PACE, LOIS, BUT I THINK LIFE IS TOO SHORT TO SIT AND WAIT.

SOMETIMES YOU HAVE TO PUSH LIFE--TAKE CHANCES. AND IF YOU FAIL--

--AT LEAST YOU CAN SAY YOU TRIED.

CHANCES? LIKE WHAT?

LIKE THIS.

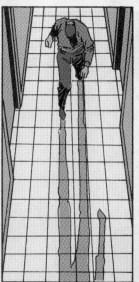

169

WELL, IT'S ABOUT TIME...

...I'VE BEEN CROUCHING OUT HERE HALF THE DAY, WAITING FOR SOMETHING TO HAPPEN!

BUT THIS IS GOING TO MAKE IT ALL WORTHWHILE!

TRUCKER HEAVEN

"JUST HOLD THAT POSE!"

KLIK-WHRR

"THANK YOU!"

"I CAN SEE THE HEADLINE NOW... ARMY MUNITIONS THIEVES CAUGHT IN THE ACT... BY LOIS LANE!"

GOTCHA!

THE QUESTION IS, WHO ARE YOU?

LET'S SEE IF WE CAN FIND OUT A LITTLE MORE, SHALL WE?

THAT'S IT?! ONLY FOUR CRATES OF M-16s AND AMMO?

THAT'S ALL I DARED SMUGGLE OUT, KELLY. THINGS ARE GETTING DICEY AT THE BASE... THE BRASS ARE STARTING TO GET WISE.

TELL MORRISON I'LL GET HIM MORE NEXT TIME. NOW GOWAN, GET OUTTA HERE!

KELLY... MORRISON... THAT'S NOT ENOUGH.

I CAN'T LET THEM SLIP AWAY FROM ME, BUT THERE'S NO TIME TO RUN BACK FOR THE CAR.

WHAT DO I DO NOW?

COME ON, LOIS, WE'RE WAITING -- JUMP!

OR DO I HAVE TO SEND ONE OF THE BOYS UP TO SHOW YOU HOW IT'S DONE?

NO WAY, DADDY DEAREST... NO WAY!

HAH! I DID IT!

LET'S SEE CLARK KENT TOP THIS!

CLARK... OH, NO! I'M AFRAID...

"... I'LL NEVER MAKE OUR DATE NOW!"

WHERE COULD SHE BE?!

SHE MISSED THE FLIGHT IN FROM METROPOLIS... AND ACCORDING TO THE RECEPTIONIST AT THE DAILY PLANET, SHE WAS OUT ALL AFTERNOON.

NONE OF OUR FRIENDS HAVE SEEN HER... THERE'S NO ANSWER AT HER APARTMENT, HER PARENTS', OR HER SISTERS'... AND MA SAYS SHE DIDN'T CALL SMALLVILLE.

MAYBE IT WAS A MISTAKE, ASKING HER TO COME HALF-WAY ACROSS THE COUNTRY FOR DINNER WITH MY PARENTS.

MAYBE SHE JUST GOT COLD FEET.

NO. NO, IF THAT WERE THE CASE, LOIS WOULD HAVE CALLED. I'M SURE SHE JUST WENT OUT AFTER A STORY, AND LOST TRACK OF TIME.

I SHOULD HEAD BACK TO SMALLVILLE. SHE'LL CALL WHEN SHE GETS THE CHANCE... UNLESS... SHE'S GOTTEN HER-SELF INTO SOME KIND OF TROUBLE!

NO, DON'T JUMP TO CONCLUSIONS! LOIS IS A VERY RESOURCEFUL, CAPABLE REPORTER... THERE'S NOT MUCH SHE CAN'T HANDLE!

BUT SHE'S NOT THE MOST CAUTIOUS PERSON IN THE WORLD!

OH, THIS IS CRAZY...

MEN

...SHE'S PROBABLY PERFECTLY ALL RIGHT, BUT NOW I'M GOING TO WORRY ABOUT HER UNTIL I KNOW FOR CERTAIN!

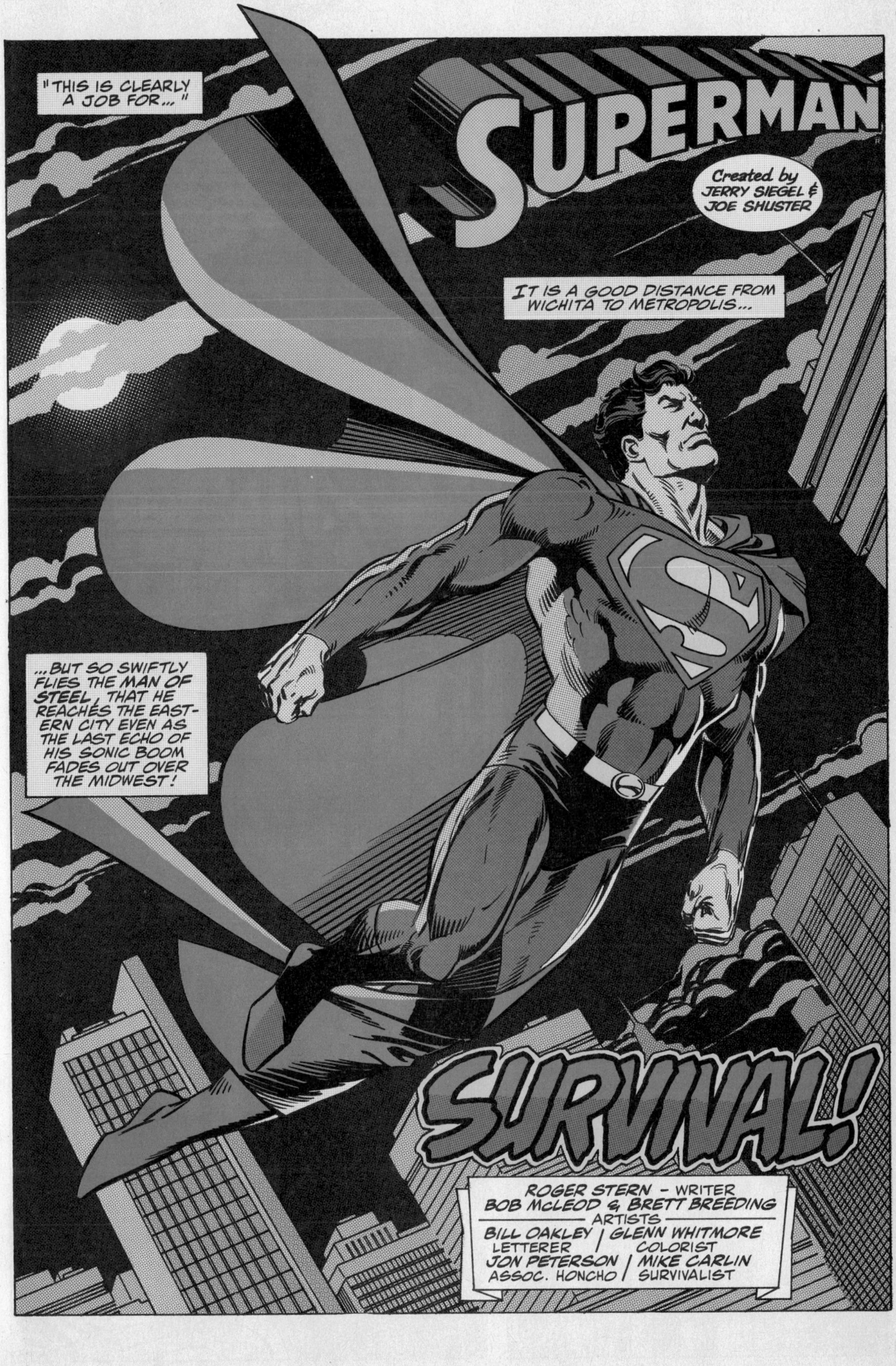
"THIS IS CLEARLY A JOB FOR..."
SUPERMAN
Created by JERRY SIEGEL & JOE SHUSTER
IT IS A GOOD DISTANCE FROM WICHITA TO METROPOLIS...
...BUT SO SWIFTLY FLIES THE MAN OF STEEL, THAT HE REACHES THE EASTERN CITY EVEN AS THE LAST ECHO OF HIS SONIC BOOM FADES OUT OVER THE MIDWEST!
SURVIVAL!
ROGER STERN - WRITER
BOB McLEOD & BRETT BREEDING
ARTISTS
BILL OAKLEY LETTERER / GLENN WHITMORE COLORIST
JON PETERSON ASSOC. HONCHO / MIKE CARLIN SURVIVALIST

WHEN I WAS IN TOWN EARLIER TODAY, I SLIPPED AND MENTIONED DINNER TO LOIS-- WHILE IN COSTUME! I DON'T THINK SHE CAUGHT IT...

...BUT AFTER I DISCOVERED THAT SHE'D MISSED HER FLIGHT, I BRIEFLY ENTERTAINED THE NOTION THAT SHE HAD STOOD CLARK UP FOR SUPERMAN.

HOW COULD I HAVE THOUGHT THAT OF LOIS? SHE'D NEVER BE SO CRUEL.

MAYBE SHE STOPPED BACK IN HERE AT THE PLANET... IT'S BEEN AWHILE SINCE I LAST CALLED--!

NO... HER DESK IS VACANT. I'M NOT SEEING ANY LINGERING HEAT IMAGES...

...NO ONE'S BEEN IN THAT CHAIR FOR AT LEAST SIX HOURS.

WHERE ARE YOU, LOIS?!

"WAIT! THERE'S AN *IMPRESSION* ON HER NOTE PAD... A NAME AND A PHONE NUMBER! IT'S VERY FAINT, BUT IF I CONCENTRATE--!"

Jake Munson
484-2851

HMM..., JAKE MUNSON. THE NAME'S NOT FAMILIAR. IT'S NOT MUCH TO GO ON--

--BUT JUST MAYBE MR. MUNSON CAN LEAD ME TO THE ELUSIVE MS. LANE.

ODD... FOR A MOMENT THERE, I HAD THE MOST DISTURBING FEELING -- WHAT WAS IT MA USED TO SAY? -- "AS IF A CAT HAD WALKED ACROSS MY GRAVE." IT'S PASSING NOW, THOUGH...

...PROBABLY JUST A REACTION TO LOIS'S DISAPPEARANCE...SURELY NOTHING TO WORRY ABOUT.

WEL-COME TO DIS-ASTER... ♪

♪ ...THE END IS DRAWING NIGH ... NO MATTER WHAT WE DO NOW...♫

♪ ...WE'RE SURELY GONNA FRY -- EEYI -- EEYI ! ♫

JIMMY...

...DO WE HAVE TO STAY HERE ?

YOU DON'T LIKE IT, HUH ?

THE BAND IS HORRIBLE, THE ROOM IS TOO SMOKY, AND... THERE'S SOMETHING ELSE ! I DON'T KNOW... MAYBE IT'S BECAUSE THIS WAS ONCE A CHURCH.

I'M NOT VERY RELIGIOUS, BUT WHAT'S BEEN DONE TO THIS PLACE IS JUST PLAIN GROSS ! DON'T YOU FEEL IT, TOO ?

YO, OLSEN !

JERRY--?

GLAD YOU MADE IT, MAN !

YOU, TOO. I DIDN'T EXPECT TO SEE YOU HERE, YOU WERE SO HYPER THIS AFTERNOON.*

OH, THAT-- I JUST HAD AN ERRAND TO RUN BEFORE MY SHIFT STARTED. HEY, WHO'S THIS PRETTY LADY ?

LUCY LANE... JERRY WHITE.

JERRY... A LITTLE OVER-DRESSED FOR THIS CLUB, AREN'T YOU ?

*IN ADVENTURES OF SUPERMAN #468, STILL ON SALE!

176

HAH! YEAH, BUT THE OWNER LIKES HER STAFF TO STAND OUT IN THE CROWD.

SO, WHAT DO YOU THINK OF BLAZE'S?

NOT MUCH.

SOMETHING WRONG? ANYTHING I COULD DO TO MAKE IT BETTER?

I SINCERELY DOUBT IT! LET'S GO, JIM.

GO? RIGHT NOW?!

WHY DON'T YOU GIVE THE PLACE A CHANCE?

YEAH, LUCE, WE REALLY JUST GOT HERE!

FINE! STAY IF YOU WANT--

--BUT DON'T EXPECT ME TO WALLOW IN IT WITH YOU!

HEY!

LUCY, WAIT!! YOU DON'T HAVE YOUR CAR! DO YOU WANT ME TO DRIVE YOU--!

DON'T PUT YOURSELF OUT! I'D RATHER WALK!

AH, LET HER GO, JIMBO! IF SHE CAN'T GET IN THE GAME, THAT'S HER LOSS!

BESIDES, THERE ARE PLENTY MORE FISH IN THIS SEA, RIGHT?

YEAH, I GUESS, BUT--!

COME ON, LET OL' JER SHOW YA HOW TO HAVE A GOOD TIME!

WELL... ALL RIGHT.

THAT'S M'MAN! AFTER ALL....

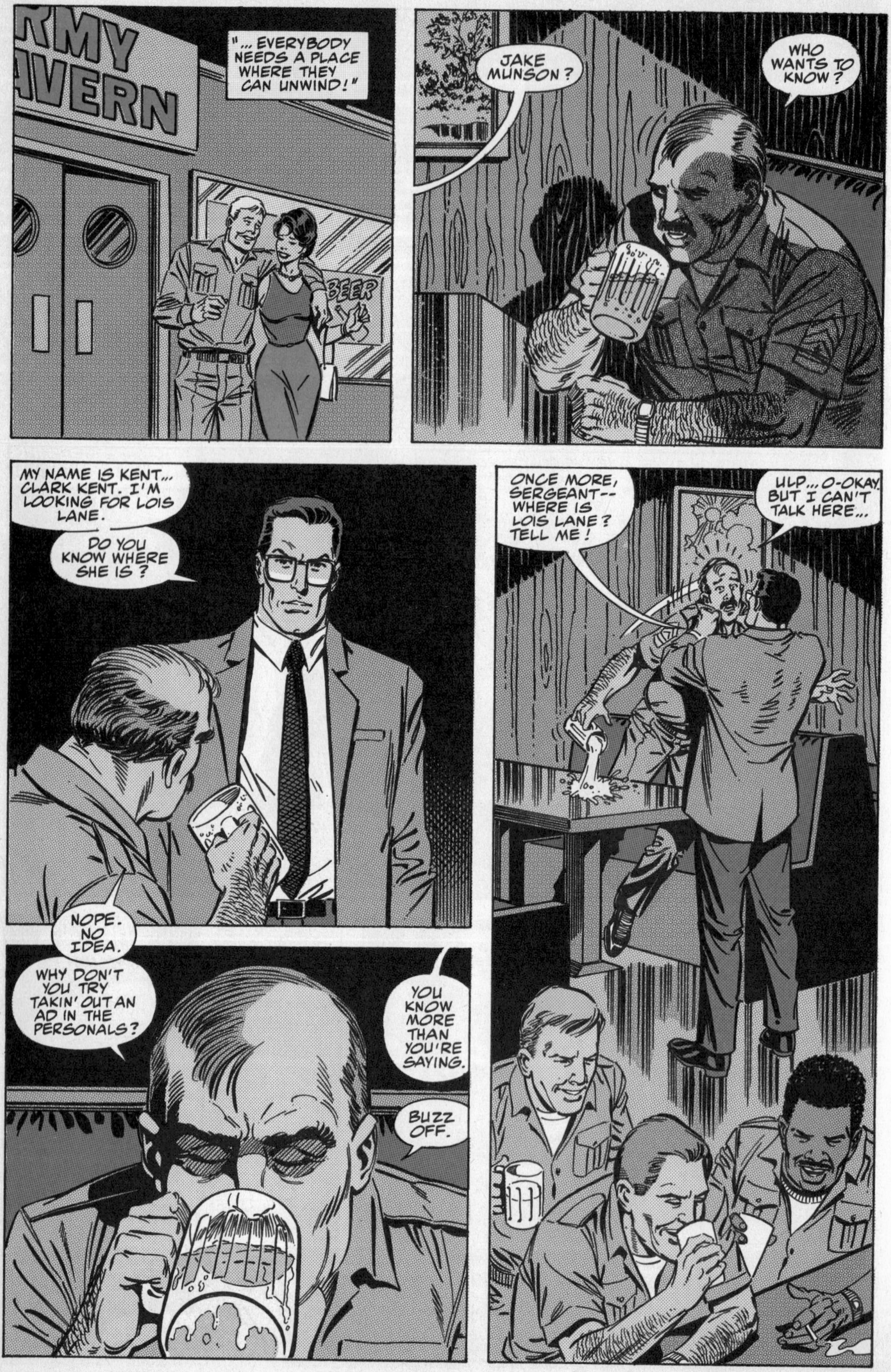
RMY
AVERN
"... EVERYBODY NEEDS A PLACE WHERE THEY CAN UNWIND!"
JAKE MUNSON?
WHO WANTS TO KNOW?
MY NAME IS KENT... CLARK KENT. I'M LOOKING FOR LOIS LANE.
DO YOU KNOW WHERE SHE IS?
NOPE. NO IDEA.
WHY DON'T YOU TRY TAKIN' OUT AN AD IN THE PERSONALS?
YOU KNOW MORE THAN YOU'RE SAYING.
BUZZ OFF.
ONCE MORE, SERGEANT-- WHERE IS LOIS LANE? TELL ME!
ULP... O-OKAY. BUT I CAN'T TALK HERE...

"...LET'S GO OUT BACK."

ALL RIGHT TALK!

SHH, NOT SO LOUD!

FIRST OFF, I DON'T KNOW WHERE THE LADY IS. BUT I HEARD O' YOU... I KNOW YOU WORK FOR THE SAME PAPER--

--SO I GUESS SHE WON'T MIND IF I TELL YOU 'BOUT HER STORY.

LOOK, LOIS WAS SUPPOSED TO MEET ME THIS EVENING AND SHE NEVER SHOWED UP. WHAT'S THIS ABOUT A STORY?

IT'S LIKE THIS... OVER THE PAST FEW MONTHS, A LOTTA HARDWARE'S GONE MISSIN' AT THE FORT-- EVERYTHING FROM SERVICE REVOLVERS ON UP TO HELICOPTER PARTS!

THE BRASS HAVE TRIED TO KEEP THINGS HUSHED UP, BUT I'M IN SUPPLY AND I HEAR A LOT OF STUFF, YA KNOW? ANYWAY, I'VE BEEN PASSIN' INFO TO THE LADY.

LAST I TALKED TO HER WAS THIS MORNIN'... SHE SAID SHE FIGURED THAT THE GEAR WAS BEIN' BOOSTED FROM SUPPLY CONVOYS AT SOME TRUCK STOP OUT ON ROUTE 100.

THAT'S ALL I KNOW, HONEST.

YOU'D BETTER BE TELLING THE TRUTH, SERGEANT.

LISTEN, KENT, I'VE KNOWN LANEY AND HER FAMILY FOR A LONG TIME! THE LAST THING I WANT IS FOR--?

KENT?

179

"WHERE THE DEVIL DID *HE GO?*"

THERE ARE DOZENS OF TRUCK STOPS ALONG ROUTE 100--

--IT COULD TAKE TAKE HOURS TO CHECK THEM ALL, BUT IT'S MY ONLY LEAD TO... *HOLD IT!*

THAT'S LUCY LANE'S CAR DOWN THERE... LOIS IS ALWAYS BORROW-ING IT WHEN HER CAR IS IN THE SHOP. I MAY HAVE JUST LUCKED OUT.

--WHOEVER MADE THEM *JUMPED! WONDERFUL.*

LOIS...

THE GROUND IS STILL SOFT FROM RECENT RAINS. FOOTPRINTS LEAD FROM THE CAR, DOWN THIS BLUFF...

...AND END *HERE!* FROM THE LOOK OF THE LAST PRINTS--

"...WHAT HAVE YOU GOTTEN YOURSELF INTO THIS TIME?"

I AM TOTALLY TURNED AROUND NOW! THE TRUCK TURNED OFF THE ROAD A GOOD THREE MILES BACK, AND I CAN'T EVEN SEE THE MOON FOR ALL OF THE TREES...

...AND THE DUST! THIS ISN'T DOING MY SINUSES ANY FAVORS!

'CHOO!

WE'RE STOPPING! UH-OH...DID THEY HEAR ME?

NO, I DON'T THINK SO. WHAT'S THAT? LOOKS LIKE SOME KIND OF --

HMMMM KLUNK

...GARAGE DOOR OPENER?

I DO NOT BELIEVE THIS!

THIS PASSAGE IS AS WIDE AS AN INTER-STATE HIGHWAY...AND IT SEEMS TO GO ON FOR MILES!

WHAT HAVE I GOTTEN MYSELF INTO THIS TIME?

OH...MY...GOD...

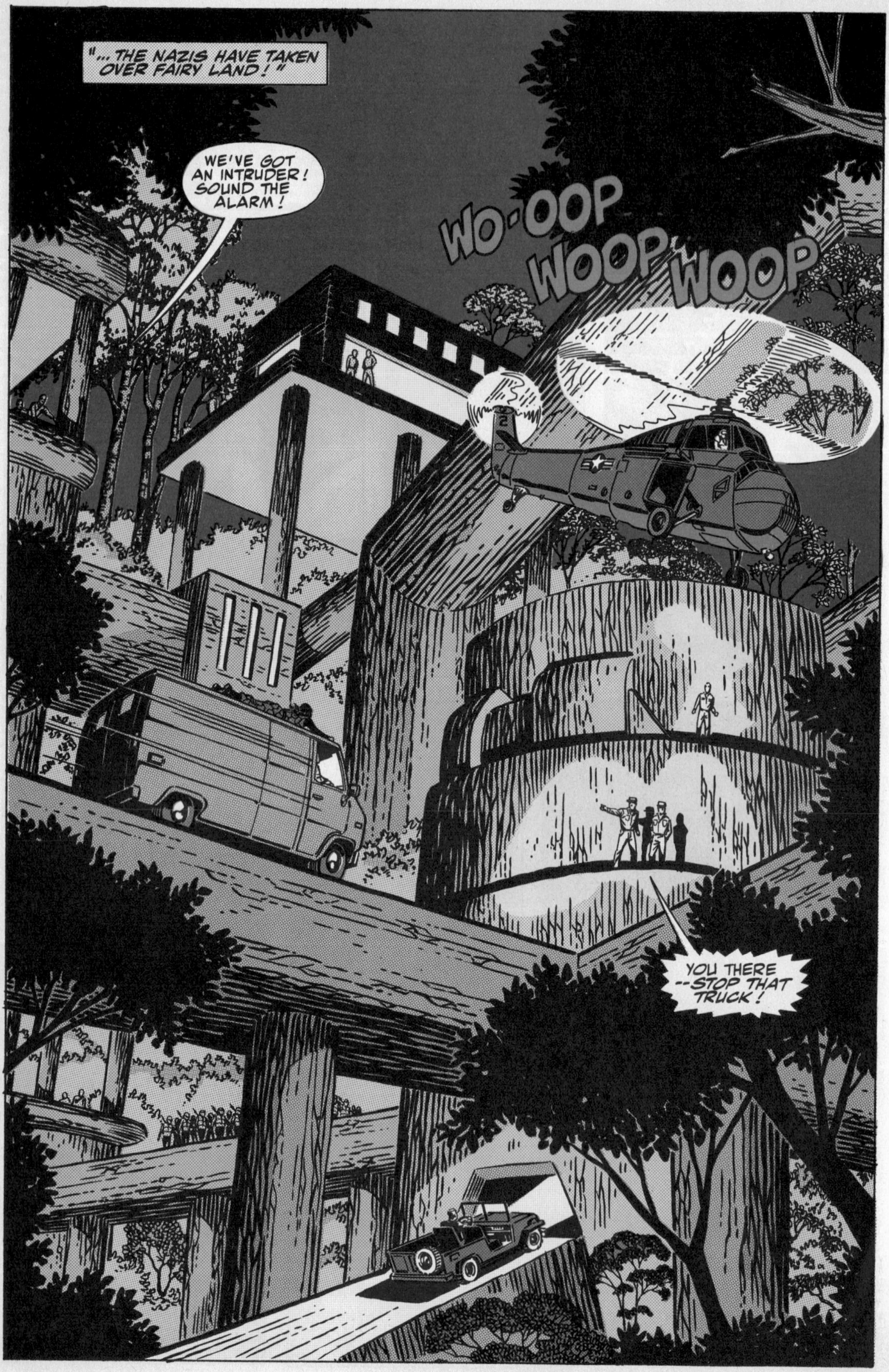
"...THE NAZIS HAVE TAKEN OVER FAIRY LAND!"
WE'VE GOT AN INTRUDER! SOUND THE ALARM!
WO-OOP WOOP WOOP
YOU THERE --STOP THAT TRUCK!

THINK FAST, LOIS!

DON'T SHOOT!

PLEASE, DON'T SHOOT! I DIDN'T MEAN TO--OWW!!

MY ANKLE! MY ANKLE!

COME ON... EASY DOES IT! ARE YOU ABLE TO STAND?

JUST FINE-- THANKS!

GAAAHH!

KRAK

FORTUNATELY, NO MAN IS STRONGER THAN HIS INSTEP!

RL 192

WHAT'S GOIN' ON OUT THERE?

THAT G#A%!! BROKE MY FOOT!

SHE WON'T GET FAR!

SAYS YOU! A FEW LIVE ROUNDS OVER THEIR HEADS SHOULD DIS-COURAGE PURSUIT--

--LONG ENOUGH FOR ME TO FIND A GOOD HOLE TO HIDE IN!

NOTHING DOWN HERE ... I'LL HAVE TO TAKE THE HIGH ROAD AND HOPE FOR THE BEST.

WHAT WAS THAT? VOICES?

OPERATION: STOCKPILE IS NEARLY COMPLETE. NOTHING WILL BE ABLE TO STOP US NOW!

OH, YEAH?

HOLD IT RIGHT... THERE.

WELL! MISS LANE, ISN'T IT?

YES, WHAT OTHER MEMBER OF THE PRESS WOULD ANNOUNCE HER ARRIVAL WITH GUNS BLAZING?

YOU SEE, I'VE BEEN TRACKING YOUR PROGRESS. COME IN, WE MUST... TALK.

"LOIS WAS NEVER ONE TO LET CAUTION GET IN THE WAY OF A STORY..."

...SHE MUST HAVE BEEN ONTO SOMETHING BIG. EVERYTHING I FOUND SUGGESTS THAT SHE JUMPED ONTO THE BACK OF A LARGE TRUCK.

AND THE MOST RECENT SET OF TIRE TRACKS NEAR THE BLUFF WHERE SHE JUMPED LED OUT OF THE PARKING AREA TO THIS BACK ROAD.

UNFORTUNATELY, THE NIGHT'S TURNING COOL... THE RESIDUAL *HEAT TRAIL* OF THE TRUCK I WANT TO FIND IS START-ING TO DISSIPATE.

A GOOD THING THERE ISN'T MUCH TRAFFIC OUT THIS WAY-- OTHERWISE, I MIGHT NEVER FIND IT.

THERE... THAT MUST BE IT! THE *HOT SPOT* ON TOP WOULD BE LOIS!

"HMMM... YES, RECENT TREAD MARKS MATCH THE ONES I FOUND BACK AT THE TRUCK STOP. BUT WHY WOULD THEY HEAD OFF DOWN THIS OLD DIRT ROAD?"

THERE'S NOTHING IN THAT DIRECTION FOR MILES AND MILES... EXCEPT...

"HABITAT, MISS LANE..."

185

...A VERITABLE CITY GROWN FROM TREES! ITS NATURAL CAMOUFLAGE PROVIDES THE PERFECT GARRISON FOR MY NEW ARMY.

HERE, WE SHALL PREPARE OURSELVES FOR ARMAGEDDON!

REALLY? WELL, TELL ME, MR. MORRISON... WHY IS IT THAT A MAN WHO CAN ENGINEER A SETUP LIKE THIS, HAS TO STEAL HIS ARMAMENT?

OH, WE DIDN'T CREATE HABITAT...

...ONE OF MY SCOUTING PARTIES FOUND IT. TO BE HONEST, I DON'T KNOW WHO MADE IT, OR WHY THEY ABANDONED IT.

THERE'S EVIDENCE THAT A SECOND HABITAT WAS CREATED NEAR NEW YORK, BUT WE'VE YET TO CONFIRM THAT.

AT ANY RATE, IT IS OURS NOW! I ONLY WISH THAT MY FATHER HAD LIVED TO SEE WHAT WE'VE ACCOMPLISHED HERE... HOW WE'VE CARRIED OUT HIS PLAN.

MY FATHER WAS A MAN OF REMARKABLE FORESIGHT, MISS LANE. HE SAW THE "END" OF THE COLD WAR FOR THE SHAM IT IS! HE KNEW THAT WE HAD TO PREPARE FOR THE ENEMY'S FINAL ASSAULT...

...TO PREPARE TO FIGHT, THAT AMERICA WOULD SURVIVE! THE ARMY I HAVE FORGED WAS HIS DREAM... A DREAM HE FOUGHT AND DIED FOR.

YOU DON'T HAVE TO TELL ME ABOUT JOHN MORRISON --

-- I RAN INTO HIM AND HIS PRIVATE ARMY ONCE.* I WASN'T IMPRESSED.

MY FATHER WAS A MAN OF GREATNESS-- OF DISCIPLINE! THAT'S SOMETHING YOU WOULD NEVER UNDERSTAND!

*IN ADVENTURES OF SUPERMAN #439.

NO. NO! NO!! HOW MANY TIMES DO I HAVE TO SHOW YOU, LOIS?! WHAT DID I DO TO DESERVE THIS?

A SON WOULD UNDERSTAND!

YOU'RE WRONG. I DO UNDERSTAND...

"...I UNDERSTAND FATHERS LIKE YOURS ALL TOO WELL!"

AS LONG AS YOU LIVE UNDER MY ROOF, YOU WILL DO THINGS MY WAY!

FINE! I COULDN'T ASK FOR A BETTER REASON TO MOVE OUT!

MY FATHER WAS AN UNAPPRECIATED GENIUS--!

YOUR FATHER WAS A RAVING PARANOID WHO BLEW HIMSELF TO KINGDOM COME!

THOOM

WHAT THE--?

RUN FOR COVER! THERE'S NO STOPPING 'IM!

MY GOD! WHAT COULD'VE DONE THAT TO A 'COPTER?

KERACK

I COULD!

SUPERMAN!!

TALK ABOUT TIMING--!

187

WHOOOAAP!

H-HALT! SURRENDER OR...OR I'LL FIRE!

NO NEED FOR THAT...

...NO NEED AND NO POINT!

WHUMP

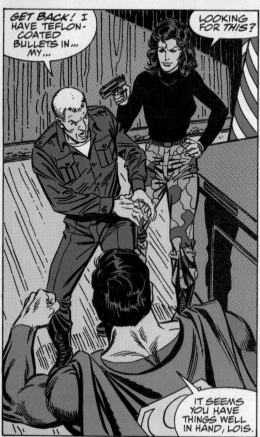

GET BACK! I HAVE TEFLON-COATED BULLETS IN... MY...

LOOKING FOR THIS?

IT SEEMS YOU HAVE THINGS WELL IN HAND, LOIS.

I DO NOW! THANKS.

I DON'T KNOW HOW YOU FOUND ME, BUT I SHOULDN'T HAVE ANY MORE TROUBLE FROM ROBIN HOOD HERE. GO ON...

"... I'LL LEAVE IT TO YOU TO ROUND UP HIS MERRY MEN!"

A DOZEN ALARMS SPLIT THE AIR, AS MEN RUSH TO ABANDON HABITAT... BUT NO MATTER WHERE THEY GO, NO MATTER WHERE THEY TURN--

-- SUPERMAN IS THERE!

ONE BY ONE, ALL AVENUES OF RETREAT ARE CUT OFF.

THE SOLDIERS OF THIS PRIVATE ARMY ARE HARDENED MEN... EX-SOLDIERS, MERCENARIES, FANATIC SUPER-PATRIOTS... DESPERATELY THEY TRY TO RESIST CAPTURE--

-- BUT THEIR WEAPONS ARE USELESS AGAINST HIM.

IN A MATTER OF MINUTES, IT IS ALL OVER.

AND SOON, IN RESPONSE TO A RADIO CALL...

ATTENTION! THIS IS MAJOR MATTHEWS OF THE 127TH AIRBORNE ARTILLERY.

COME ON DOWN, MAJOR!

SUPERMAN SAID TO GIVE YOU HIS REGRETS. TOO BAD YOU MISSED OUT ON ALL OF THE FUN!

YOU WANT TO SIGN FOR THESE JERKS?

MORNING...

WHAT DO YOU MEAN, "TOP SECRET"?!?

CHIEF, I RISKED MY NECK TO UNCOVER THE PARTY BEHIND THOSE MUNITIONS THEFTS! DON'T TELL ME MY STORY'S KILLED BECAUSE THE ARMY WANTS TO COVER ITS COLLECTIVE BEHIND?!

IT'S NOT LIKE THAT, LOIS...

THANKS TO YOUR WORK, THE ARMY IS NO LONGER DENYING THE THEFTS. BUT COL. BOGART SAYS THERE'S A SECURITY MATTER IN THE MIX.

SECURITY?!

CORRECT, MS. LANE. HABITAT IS THE OFFSHOOT OF A CLASSIFIED PROJECT.* ITS EXISTENCE MUST BE KEPT AS MUCH A SECRET AS POSSIBLE.

*KNOWN TO LONGTIME READERS AS THE CADMUS PROJECT!

YOU ARE, OF COURSE, FREE TO RUN YOUR STORY ABOUT MORRISON'S SURVIVALISTS AND THEIR THEFTS... AS LONG AS HABITAT IS NOT MENTIONED AND NO PHOTOS OF THE AREA ARE RUN.

I DON'T LIKE IT ANY MORE THAN YOU DO, LOIS--

--BUT HALF A LOAF IS BETTER THAN NONE.

ACTUALLY, MS. LANE, THE ARMY OWES YOU A DEBT...

DON'T MENTION IT, COLONEL.

SHORTLY...

'MORNING, EARLY BIRD!

CLARK! WHAT'RE YOU--? THAT'S LUCY'S CAR! HOW DID YOU--?

WHOA! ONE QUESTION AT A TIME, OKAY?

SUPERMAN TOLD ME YOU'D GOTTEN DELAYED ON A STORY... AND THAT YOU'D HAD TO LEAVE YOUR SISTER'S CAR OUT IN THE COUNTRY.

I THOUGHT I'D BRING IT BACK FOR YOU.

CLARK, ABOUT LAST NIGHT--! I'M SORRY... THE STORY GOT AWAY FROM ME... I LOST TRACK OF TIME AND--!

HEY, IT'S ALL RIGHT.

I'M A REPORTER, TOO, REMEMBER? SEEMS TO ME THAT I'VE KEPT YOU WAITING ON MORE THAN ONE OCCASION.

HOWEVER, IF YOU MUST APOLOGIZE, YOU MIGHT AS WELL DO IT ON A FULL STOMACH. I KNOW A LITTLE DOCKSIDE CAFÉ THAT DOES A GREAT BREAKFAST.

CLARK KENT, YOU ARE REALLY SOMETHING ELSE...

...MMM-MWAH!! AND I AM FAMISHED! LET'S GO!

The End

191

The Thrilling Legend of the Man of Steel
Continues in These DC Books:

COSMIC ODYSSEY
Jim Starlin / Mike Mignola / Carlos Garzon

WORLD'S FINEST
Dave Gibbons / Steve Rude / Karl Kesel

LEGENDS: THE COLLECTED EDITION
John Ostrander / Len Wein / John Byrne / Karl Kesel

THE MAN OF STEEL
John Byrne / Dick Giordano

SUPERMAN: PANIC IN THE SKY
Various Writers and Artists

SUPERMAN: THE DEATH OF SUPERMAN
Various Writers and Artists

SUPERMAN: WORLD WITHOUT A SUPERMAN
Various Writers and Artists

SUPERMAN: THE RETURN OF SUPERMAN
Various Writers and Artists

Coming Soon

SUPERMAN: TIME AND TIME AGAIN